The Explorer's Gazette

AMAZING STORIES OF 30 REAL-LIFE JOURNEYS

BY MELISSA HECKSCHER, MARK SHULMAN, AND THE STAFF OF *THE EXPLORER'S GAZETTE*

The Explorer's Gazette

ESTABLISHED 327 B.C.

PUBLISHER
Sharyn Rosart

EDITOR-IN-CHIEF
Melissa Heckscher

STAFF WIT
Mark Shulman

STAFF HISTORIANS
Johan Gunk, Gregory Page

STAFF UNUSUAL "HOW-TO" AUTHORITIES
Professor Benjamin Bundt, Professor Harry N. Fast, Will Float, Professor Churchill Garbanzo, Dr. Star E. Gazer, Wiley Noise, Monocle Tati, Professor Antoine Square, Alan Stamps, Professor Wheezy West, Jenkins Yukon

STAFF HOLIDAY HOUNDS
Cheryl Cherub, Cort Jesters

STAFF FOOD FANS
Esther, Salty C. Rancher

STAFF OPINION SHARERS
Chaz Aztec, Lotte Baloney, Fido Barks, Walt A. Crock, Xerxes Hammond

STAFF FUTURE SEER
Opticus

MANAGING EDITORS
Sarah Scheffel & Paige Araujo

ART DIRECTOR
Lynne Yeamans

PRODUCTION DIRECTOR
Bill Rose

DESIGNERS
Sue Livingston & Nancy Leonard

PHOTO EDITOR
Erika Rubel

ILLUSTRATORS
Nancy Leonard & Raina Telgemeier

COPY EDITOR
Amy Vinchesi

EDITOR-AT-LARGE
Tricia Levi

Copyright© 2004 by Quirk Packaging, Inc.
www.quirkpackaging.com

Scholastic and Tangerine Press and associated logos are trademarks of Scholastic Inc.

Published by Tangerine Press, an imprint of Scholastic Inc.
557 Broadway
New York, NY 10012

10 9 8 7 6 5 4 3 2 1

ISBN 0-439-67653-3

Printed and bound in China

an imprint of
SCHOLASTIC
www.scholastic.com

The Explorer's Gazette

INTRODUCTION

WHERE WOULD WE BE WITHOUT EXPLORERS?

Imagine that you have just heard an amazing story about a magical place where candy bars grow on trees. Supposedly, it is *very* far from home. Would you go off in search of this mysterious candy land?

Not so long ago brave people traveled vast distances to unknown places (in search of much more important things than candy-bearing trees). They didn't know what they would find and much about where they were going. Often, they just had a general direction. They didn't even know how big the oceans were—or if the world was round or flat! They didn't know who or what they would find when they got to their destinations. In other words, they didn't know a lot—

and that was the point. Exploring was—and is still—all about discovering and answering questions about our world and universe.

For more than two millennia, *The Explorer's Gazette* has been covering the amazing stories of the intrepid adventurers who have changed the world. Our staff of ace reporters has trudged to the ends of the Earth, the bottoms of the oceans, and the edges of the universe, following the men and women who sought to get there first.

In 1934, when William Beebe plunged into the sea outside Bermuda, he didn't know what to expect of the ocean's never-before-seen depths, but he did it anyway. When Buzz Aldrin and Neil Armstrong took off from

Earth in 1969 to become the first men to land on the moon, they knew the risks but weren't deterred.

Ferdinand Magellan didn't live to see the end of his around-the-world voyage in 1522, but it was his direction that made the historic journey possible.

The staff of *The Explorer's Gazette*, which, in addition to reporters, includes editors, scientists, and other experts, has covered history's most celebrated explorers. What is the one simple quality they share? Courage. They all had the courage to face the unknown.

But what leads people to explore?

Sometimes, they want to test how brave they are. Edmund Hillary and Tenzing Norgay endured

a steep, perilous climb and frigid temperatures to reach the summit of Mount Everest in 1953. Sometimes, it is to make the world a better place. Meriwether Lewis's and William Clark's exploration to the Pacific Coast of the United States paved the way for thousands—and later, millions—of Americans to settle the West.

The amazing adventurers featured in the pages of *The Explorer's Gazette* over the ages have made it possible to better understand our world and our universe. After all, if these brave people hadn't gone first, we would never have known what was out there.

PHOTO CREDITS

THE Explorer's Gazette

JUNE 10, 323 B.C.   VOLUME CCCXXIII No. 24   PRICE: ONE SILVER TETRADRACHM

HE'S GONE! ALEXANDER ENDS LIFETIME OF GREATNESS

Ten-month-old son next in line to lead

Alexander III

MACEDONIA – Alexander III, the king of Macedonia and Persia, and the man known as one of the best war generals in history, died yesterday at the age of 33 after more than a decade of battles, explorations, and countless victories.

Alexander, who has come to be known as "Alexander the Great" for his triumphant military career, which left him in control of much of the modern world, took to the throne at the

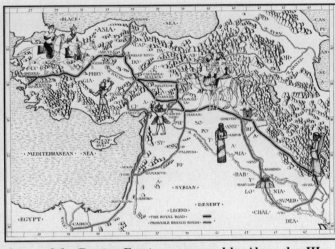

Areas of the Persian Empire conquered by Alexander III.

age of 20 after the mysterious murder of his father.

Despite his young age, Alexander was prepared to be a king. As a child he had received the best education possible. He studied with the renowned philosopher Aristotle, who was his personal tutor. Consequently, moving from teenage prince-hood to fearless leader was an easy transition. Shortly after becoming king, he proved himself worthy of the title by quieting the warring

cities of Greece and calming military uprisings in Thrace and Illyria.

At the age of 22, Alexander followed his father's plans to go to war with Persia. With a powerful and unified Greek army marching, the battle was one of the greatest that was ever seen. Alexander emerged victorious. At that point Alexander was determined to conquer the entire Persian Empire, a vast empire that controlled an area from India to Greece.

IN RECENT NEWS

Greeks believe "Breathing Earth" causes tides. See WEATHER.

Philosopher Aristotle proves Earth is round. See WORLD NEWS.

Homer publishes *The Odyssey* and *The Iliad*; both books destined to become classics. See LITERATURE.

Within two years he had conquered Tyre, Gaza, Syria, and Egypt. By the age of 25, Alexander controlled all the countries in the eastern Mediterranean region. Some said he was planning to conquer the whole world.

"He was unstoppable," said one of Alexander's soldiers. "When we marched toward those cities, he had complete

(continued on page 2)

Alexander III, otherwise known as Alexander the Great, preparing for a fight. A land-hungry man, he spent one-third of his life leading battles.

(continued from page 1)

confidence that we were going to win. We always won."

Winning must have gotten to Alexander's head. While he was in Egypt, he was acknowledged as the son of Amon-Ra, a great god. According to *Explorer's Gazette* sources, he even began to consider himself immortal.

"Many of the Greeks really resented him for this," said Athens resident Alexis Xerxes. "He expected to be treated like a god, but he was only a man."

"With numerous victories under his belt, Alexander thought nothing could hurt him," said Greek professor Leon Phoenicia. "He thought nothing could stop him."

But something did. After conquering Northern Africa, Afghanistan, and India, Alexander's power weakened. By that time his army had lost some of its might, and there was word many of his soldiers were planning to revolt.

"Maybe he knew things were going downhill and he couldn't take it," said Phoenicia. "He wanted to end while he was still on top."

Sources said the great king developed a fever in Babylon and died inside the palace of Nebuchadnezzar II. His 10-month-old son Alexander is now the rightful emperor.

Aristotle: Wise Man Taught Alexander the Great

By Gregory Page

Alexander III was privileged to have the thinker Aristotle as his teacher. A philosopher, educator, and scientist, Aristotle is considered one of the most influential thinkers in the world today.

Born in northern Greece the son of a doctor, Aristotle was trained first in medicine; however, at age 17 he was sent to Athens to study philosophy with celebrated philosopher Plato.

Aside from his work in philosophy, Aristotle is also renowned because of his system for classifying plants and animals into distinct categories, called generas and species. In fact, while Alexander was traveling through Western Asia, he often sent unfamiliar plants to Aristotle so he could study them. It is thought that Aristotle's classification system will be used to name plants and animals for centuries to come.

Aristotle also developed many theories on the workings of the Earth, including the idea for the hydrologic cycle ("the water cycle"), the theory that says all water on the Earth is continuously recycled, with the rain deposited in oceans and streams eventually evaporating into air and becoming rain again.

He is also one of the first to propose that the Earth is round, and not flat, a fact still disputed by many scientists and citizens alike.

THE EXPLORER'S GAZETTE

SEPTEMBER 19, 1001   VOLUME MI No. 38   PRICE: ONE SILVER PENNY

LIKE FATHER, LIKE SON

Leif Eriksson, son of Erik the Red, has also found a New World

Leif Eriksson sails from his home in Greenland and finds a fertile new land with many natural resources. It's warm, too!

VINLAND, NORTH AMERICA – Like most Viking explorers, Leif Eriksson didn't need a map to get where he was going.

The adventurer, the son of notorious explorer Erik the Red, recently returned home after becoming the first European to set foot on a lush new land about 600 miles (960 km) southwest of Greenland. According to *Explorer's Gazette* sources, that new land is part of a larger continent that will one day be called North America.

"This is a monumental discovery," said Greenland ice fisherman Jaquin Frederickson. "As opposed to the cold, icy conditions on Greenland, this land is ripe for living. Leif has found us a paradise."

Finding paradise came naturally for Eriksson, who has the spirit of exploration in his blood. His father, Erik the Red (so named for his full head of red hair) founded the country of Greenland after he was exiled from Iceland.

The largest island in the world, located northwest of Iceland, in the Arctic Ocean, Greenland is far from green;

(continued on page 2)

LIFE ON A VIKING SHIP

By Johan Gunk

Viking longships aren't the most comfortable method of travel. Long, open boats with no covered quarters, they offer no protection from the elements. Because of this, Vikings do not make voyages in winter and generally wait until the spring to set sail. Even so, the climate is often chilly and the voyages rough.

Sleeping: When conditions allow, Vikings pull ashore at night and take down the sail to create a tent to sleep under. If the crew is far out to sea, they have to sleep on the open deck beneath blankets or sleeping bags made of animal skin.

Food: At sea Vikings live mostly on dried meat or salted fish. Food can only be cooked if the sailors are able to land. If they are at sea, the food is never cooked, for they cannot risk setting the ship on fire for the sake of a hot meal.

Drink: Vikings must transport fresh water, beer, or sour milk on their journeys.

(continued from page 1)

about 84 percent of it is covered by ice. Erik named the country Greenland only to make it seem attractive to potential settlers. The ploy worked, and about 3,000 settlers established colonies there.

It was Erik's discovery of Greenland that led to his son's recent discovery. Erik had heard of a sailor named Bjarni who had gotten lost and seen land southwest of Greenland. He had never pulled ashore but returned to Greenland telling stories of a distant land marked by faraway hills and thick forests.

Leif was intrigued. He bought Bjarni's longship, a typical Viking ship with sweeping oars and square sails, and set out. After five days battling frigid waters, he and his 35-man crew reached the mysterious land Bjarni had seen.

Pulling ashore, they were disappointed, for the land seemed to be one ongoing rock slab. He named the area Helluland, which means land of flat stones. Turning southward, he then found a coastline with white sand beaches bounded by dense forest. He named it Markland, or Woodland.

He finally arrived at a third location, which tempted the Vikings with fertile grazing ground and plenty of timber and salmon. He chose to name that area Vinland, or "Vineland the Good," after the many giant grape vines that grow naturally there.

"He and his men returned to Greenland telling of this rich, fertile land with beautiful coastlines and grapes growing without the aid of farming," said Iceland resident Garf Gustaphson. "We all want to sail back with him."

And they might. Already, dozens of expeditions are being planned to explore and colonize the land, which, according to *Explorer's Gazette* sources, will one day be called Newfoundland.

A map of Leif Eriksson's homeland, the icy cold (and foolishly named) Greenland.

How to Navigate Following the North Star

By Professor Churchill Garbanzo

Vikings don't use maps to navigate the seas. Instead they follow the sun and stars, the color of the sea, the motion of the waves, and the documented warnings of other Vikings.

The North Star, also known as Polaris, is a very bright star visible in the night skies of the Northern Hemisphere, and an important navigational tool because the axis of the earth points directly at it. Here's how you can find it:

Directly overhead you will find a constellation of seven stars that looks like a dipping cup; that's the Big Dipper. Follow the two rightmost stars—known as the "Pointer Stars"—upward to Polaris, which is at the end of the handle of the Little Dipper (see diagram).

Aiming your ship (or your feet) toward Polaris will take you to the North Pole and closer to all points north. Once you know north, you can figure out the other three directions: south, east, and west.

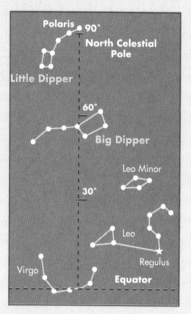

In My Crystal Ball

By Opticus, Seer of All Things Future

I PREDICT . . . In 1002 many immigrants will arrive in Greenland, but the icy land will never be densely populated . . . Leif Erikson will inherit his father's position as leader of Greenland . . . About 400 years later, North America will be colonized by Europeans and eventually become its own nation . . . Leif will one day be recognized as the first European to set foot in the New World.

THE EXPLORER'S GAZETTE

JANUARY 9, 1324   VOLUME MCCCXXIV No. 2   PRICE: ONE GOLD FLORIN

MARCO POLO: ELABORATE STORYTELLER OR ACCOMPLISHED EXPLORER?

After death of renowned traveler, many still question truth of Marco Polo's tales

PROS AND CONS

THAT POLO IS A FRAUD!

By Lotte Baloney

Marco Polo is indeed "The Man of a Million Lies," I say. He has come back from China with many stories, yes. But many of us believe he is taking credit for the tales of other travelers. Why does his book not mention the everyday use of chopsticks or tea? Or beautiful Chinese calligraphy (handwriting) or The Great Wall of China? Why are they missing? I think it's *because Marco never went to China!*

Marco Polo

VENICE, ITALY – Some people would call Marco Polo a traveling genius, a man who toured the world and brought back colorful tales of faraway places. Some people would say his tales of distant lands were vivid enough to carry them away, if only in their imaginations.

And some people would say he made it all up.

Now the world may never know for sure. The renowned merchant, adventurer, and traveler, who had been voyaging from Europe to Asia and the Middle East since he was a child, died yesterday at the age of 70.

For most of his life Polo was a world traveler. He began traveling at the age of 14, when his father, Niccolo, and uncle, Matteo, took him along on their exotic sea voyages. The men journeyed to Jerusalem, Armenia, Persia, Afghanistan, the Pamir mountains, and along the Silk Road to China.

"They went by foot, by horse, by boat. They even rode a raft of inflated pigskins," said 12-year-old Mario LeStorio, one of the many Italian youths enthralled by Polo's stories. "I wish my dad would take me on those kinds of journeys."

As an adult Polo's travels were focused primarily on Asia. He spent about 16 years based

(continued on page 2)

Hard to stamp: Polo was given a golden "passport" by the Kublai Khan. This enabled him to travel anywhere throughout Asia. The gold tablet also entitled him to free food, lodging, and guides wherever he traveled throughout the kingdom.

Marco Polo arrives in northern China.

Some of his accounts remain unchallenged, however. He obviously went to exotic lands, and the proof existed in the artifacts he brought back, including various foods and articles of clothing. His discoveries of pasta, especially spaghetti, and of ice cream were the most popular of his faraway findings; the foods became instant favorites throughout Italy.

"I don't care whether he made stories up here and there," said Italian philosopher Leonardo B. Leevpolo. "He got some things right. You can taste it."

According to some *Explorer's Gazette* sources, Polo insisted he was telling the truth, right up until the very end. On his deathbed, he was asked by a priest if he had faked stories. His reply: "I did not tell half of what I saw."

(continued from page 1)

there while exploring much of China, where he reportedly became a favorite of the notorious Mongol leader Kublai Khan and worked as a tax collector for the Chinese government.

He scoured the land, picking up things along the way, writing down his observations, and bringing home very detailed accounts of the amazing things he saw. In his book *Il Milione*, or *The Travels of Marco Polo*, Polo described the remarkable inventions of his Chinese hosts, including how they use coal for heat; how they use printed paper for money; how they make silk from worm threads; and how they use gunpowder to make weapons.

But more than anything else, Polo brought back stories. Lots of them. In fact, he told so many stories that many people began to think he was making them up, or that he was exaggerating what he saw into more fantastical tales to entertain his listeners.

"For one thing, his stories failed to mention the unique utensils they use and their special drink," said Venice professor Milo Cynicio. "How could he visit China and not tell about them?"

"He talked about so many things that sounded so unbelievable," added Venice Resident Gippetto Pastananni. "They were great stories, but maybe that's all they were."

In My Crystal Ball

By Opticus, *Seer of All Things Future*

I PREDICT . . . for centuries, mapmakers and travelers will find Marco Polo's book highly accurate . . . Henry the Navigator and Christopher Columbus will read it closely for valuable clues . . . it will be the most-read travel book for 600 years . . . and in honor of his wanderings a children's game shall be named "Marco Polo."

Make the Noodles of China!

The restaurants of China won't deliver food all the way to Venice. So here's how you can make a bowl of Polo's pasta for yourself. (Make sure you've got an adult with you to help.)

> 2 eggs
> 1½ cups (360 ml) flour (and possibly more)
> Teaspoon of salt

1. Make a mound with the flour on a flat, dry surface. Make a well in the center of the mound. Beat the eggs and pour them into the well. Start mixing the eggs and flour together with a fork, holding the sides of the mound with your free hand.

2. When the mixture begins to get solid, get rid of the fork and start mixing with your hands. Before long you'll have a workable dough, which should be kneaded with your hands for several minutes. The dough should be smooth and stretchy, not sticky or stiff. (Dust the dough with flour as necessary if it's too sticky.)

3. Roll out the dough into a sheet about ⅛-inch (3 mm) thick. Let the sheet dry for 30 minutes. Cut the dough into thin strips for spaghetti or slightly thicker strips for linguine.

4. To prepare fresh pasta, add the dried and cut strips to boiling water and cook for 4 minutes, stirring occasionally. Drain the pasta in a colander set in the sink. Serve with your favorite sauce.

THE EXPLORER'S GAZETTE

JULY 1355   VOLUME MCCCLV No. 29   PRICE: ONE GOLD FLORIN

AFTER ALMOST 30 YEARS, IBN BATTUTA RETURNS TO MOROCCO

Journey home spans dozens of countries, thousands of miles

Ibn Battuta, his crew, and their boats (called dhows) being attacked by pirates.

TANGIER, MOROCCO – Capping off what began as a simple pilgrimage to Mecca and became a cross-continental journey, Ibn Battuta arrived home this week after an almost 30-year trek that spanned dozens of countries and about 75,000 miles (120,000 km).

The 2,900-mile (4,700-km) route between Tangier and Mecca, a journey traveled by Moslems who consider it to be a sacred passage, normally takes about six months. Most travelers return home after reaching Mecca, but Battuta wanted to explore further.

"When he reached Mecca and had finished his *hajj*, his sacred journey, he thought to himself, 'There's probably a different road home to Morocco,'" said Mustapha Qontrac, a friend and advisor. "As it turned out, his road was a much, much longer way home."

Battuta, who described the voyage as the most exciting

IN RECENT NEWS

Renaissance begins, Dark Ages come to an end. See BIG CHANGES.

"Ring-Around-the-Rosy" inspired by the death of one-third of Europe's population from the bubonic plague. See GAMES.

Kitchen fire pits voted "favorite way to cook at home." See FOOD.

journey of his life, made the trek wearing only sandals to protect his feet from the often harsh terrain. He began the journey in 1325, at the age of 21. Since then, he has walked through every Moslem nation in the world.

According to sources, Battuta was recently asked by the Sultan of Morocco to write about his travels. The book,

(continued on page 2)

What's in a Name?

The editors at *The Explorer's Gazette* voted on their favorite-sounding Batutta destination.

THE FINALISTS: Aden, Aleya, Balkh, Hormuz, Goa, Khawarism, Kulwa, Kambay, Malwah, Mashhad, Nishapur, Seraf, Sinope, Tus, Yamama.

AND THE WINNER IS: Yamama (a coastal town in Saudi Arabia).

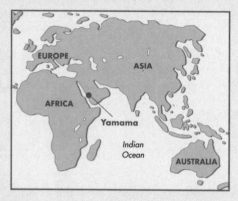

Droopy Dromedary?

Is your camel depressed? Not getting enough exercise?

Abdul's Exercise Plan can get your beast over the hump.

"I'll walk a camel for a mile."

ASK A STRANGER

Where would you go if you traveled 75,000 miles?

"I'd go to the river 150,000 times."
—Marcus Ishdad, musician, age 17

"I'd go one-third of the way to the moon. Or one-sixth of the way, round trip."
—Dr. Bugnatious Nann, astronomer, age 37

"I'd go crazy."
—Jonah Meeks, hairdresser, age 25

(continued from page 1)

which will be called, *Rihla [Travels] of Ibn Battuta*, will recount Battuta's many years of wandering.

And there are hundreds of stories to tell. During those thirty years abroad, Battuta visited about 44 countries throughout Africa, the Middle East, the Far East, and Europe. He had several different wives and many children. He saw a kaleidoscope of different cultures, clothing, people, and landscapes.

"Most of us will never get the chance to visit these places, but Battuta's stories are enough to take you there, at least in your imagination," said 16-year-old Isiah Mamoun, one of many Moroccans to hear Battuta's tales of faraway places. "He was very brave to spend his life moving from place to place like that."

Moving was what he did best. Battuta traveled by caravan throughout the Middle East and sailed by ship up and down the African coasts. He worked for the Sultan of Delhi in India and traveled with one of his wives to her native country of Turkey, where another Sultan hired him as a judge and later as the Turkish Ambassador to China.

His travels weren't free of danger. He was attacked by bandits; he almost drowned in a sinking ship; and once a tyrant ruler tried to have him beheaded.

But it wasn't all perilous. In the Maldive Islands, a cluster of islands southwest of Sri Lanka, Battuta was named chief judge and was given the privilege of marrying an island princess.

"He had time for romance," Qontrac pointed out. "You see, it wasn't all robberies and danger."

Whether it was the lure of romance or the thrill of adventure, Battuta seems addicted to the traveling life. After spending just four days in his home of Tangier, he has already announced his next journey. This time Battuta said he plans on exploring Spain, Morocco, the Sahara, and West Africa.

The always-on-the-go Battuta with a native man.

THE Explorer's Gazette

DECEMBER 1435   VOLUME MCDXXXV No. 50   PRICE: TWO GOLD FLORINS

HE SAILED, HE SAW, HE CONQUERED

ZHENG HE, CHINA'S GREATEST OCEAN EXPLORER, DIES DURING SEVENTH VOYAGE

NANJING, CHINA – Zheng He, a man who has been called China's greatest ocean explorer and is said to have circled the entire earth by water, died recently during his seventh voyage after a lifetime of travel.

"He died as he would have wanted it—in the middle of a journey," said Chin Lee, a friend of Zheng's. "He was always in the middle of an adventure."

Zheng's adventures began almost the moment he was born. Given the name Ma He in 1371, he was kidnapped as a child and sent to be a servant in the home of the current emperor's fourth son, Prince Zhu Di. In 1402, when Zhu Di rose to become a Ming emperor himself, he renamed his intelligent and diplomatic servant Zheng, a name that would give him higher status in Chinese society.

Zhu Di had big ideas for Zheng. According to a source

Zheng He's Treasure Fleet is the largest-ever group of ships sailing together.

in the Ming family, the Emperor instructed Zheng to build more than 300 ships, take 30,000 men with him, and open trade with India, Africa, and beyond.

Zheng followed his orders perfectly. Three years later the world's largest fleet, called the Treasure Fleet, was launched with Zheng He in command.

"It was the largest fleet the world had ever seen," said Lee. "Nobody would dare stand

up to such an army. It was massive."

The enormous fleet included ships measuring more than 400 feet (125 meters) long and 150 feet (47 meters) wide, with nine masts and sails each. The armada included warships, troop ships, supply ships and water ships. In addition there were horse ships for cavalry, and bull ships for fresh meat.

From 1405 to 1433, Zheng made a total of nine monumen-

IN RECENT NEWS

Europe reportedly developing "Printing Press" to reproduce copies of books and images. See INNOVATIONS.

University of Oxford making final preparations to open in England. See EDUCATION.

Portugal's Gil Eanes set to explore coast of West Africa. See NEW LANDS.

tal voyages, with his primary mission to make maps of uncharted territories and develop trading relationships with other countries.

His journeys were full of adventures. He captured the king of Sri Lanka, attacked the country of Mogadishu, and helped invade Calicut, India. And while Zheng was described as a confident warrior, the ocean itself may have been his biggest opponent: it held the peril of raging storms,

(continued on page 2)

(continued from page 1)

thieving pirates, and endless expanses of unknown waters.

Using a Chinese invention called a compass, as well the constellations in the night sky, Zheng's fleets sailed farther than any other nation's ships. Evidence of his accomplishments may one day be found in the lands of Australia, the Caribbean, and the West Coast of North America.

"Zheng's journeys established China as the world's top naval power," said Lee. "He should be remembered for centuries as a leader in seafaring exploration."

But he may not be, if the current emperor has his way. According to sources, Emperor Hongxi, a member of the long-reigning Ming dynasty, recently seized China's entire fleet and ordered that travel abroad be illegal. It is unclear why Hongxi gave these orders, but a source described him as "merciless."

"He doesn't want China mixing with the world and says naval exploration is a waste of money," said a former Treasure Fleet crew member who didn't want to be identified. "He even destroyed all of Zheng He's maps and records!"

Will Zheng He be forgotten? Surely not. Sources say some of his sailors took notes, hid maps, and sailed the last boat out of China.

"His life was too important to be forgotten," said Lee. "We will remember him."

In My Crystal Ball

By Opticus, *Seer of All Things Future*

I PREDICT . . . Despite the Emperor's wishes, a few of Zheng He's maps and star charts will survive . . . Dias, Columbus, Magellan, and Cook will admit to having maps of "unexplored" waters . . . many will think these are He's maps . . . China will be the superpower in the Indian Ocean until the 1500s, when Portugal sets up their colonies along the ocean route to India.

Did You Know?

With Professor Wheezy West

"True north" is a human concept. "Magnetic north" gets its power from the magnetic pull of the North Pole. That's what affects the needle of a compass. Magnetic north is different in different parts of the world, depending on the distance from the North Pole. For most of North and South America and Europe, the difference is no more than 20 degrees (the compass says "north" but it's really pointing "northwest"). Guess what? Even if you're lost at sea, that's close enough to find land.

How to Make a Compass

The Chinese reportedly invented the compass. Now you can find your way to making one too.

1. Place a sewing needle on a strong magnet for 30 minutes to absorb the magnet's charge.

2. Find a small, flat piece of cork no bigger than a dime.

3. Float the cork in a small bowl of water and lay the needle on the cork. The needle will point to magnetic north! (See **Did You Know?** to find out why.)

YOUR WORLD, CHANGING WITH EVERY EXPEDITION

The Explorer's Gazette

July 1488   Volume MCDLXXXVII No. 29   Price: TWO GOLD FLORINS

PORTUGAL TAKES AFRICA BY STORM

Raging storms can't stop Dias and crew from reaching tip of Africa; new trade routes proposed

Statue of Bartolomeu Dias

LISBON, PORTUGAL – Portugal's own Bartolomeu Dias, with brothers Pero and Diogo, took the first modern European expedition around the lower tip of Africa earlier this month, a dangerous undertaking for sailors given the area's reputation for tumultuous seas and raging storms.

The brothers were sent on the perilous journey by Portugal's former Prince Henry "The Navigator," who wanted the adventurers to make new maps, find foreign spices, and discover a speedy sea route to India along Africa's coast.

In addition to the Dias brothers, notorious adventurers Gil Eannes and Vasco Da Gama were along for the voyage.

"It's no wonder Portugal is fast becoming the world's naval superpower," said 17-year-old Jose DeJamba, an aspiring sailor. "These men were brave for battling those seas."

Over the years many have faced Africa's fierce storms and unpredictable currents, often without success. With the cold ocean current on the west coast meeting the warm Agulhas current from the east, the renowned horn of Africa has intimidated many voyagers, and many ships have been lost.

Conquering the region will mean opening up a new and more direct pathway around Africa, which will help future trade and exploration.

"All that was standing in Portugal's way were these

King John II of Portugal

IN RECENT NEWS

Leonardo DaVinci seeks volunteers to test newly invented "parachute." See TECHNOLOGY.

Mathematicians work with new "plus" and "minus" signs. See INNOVATIONS.

Spanish use first ambulances; doctors hope speedy transportation will deliver sick to hospitals and clinics before it's too late. See HEALTH & MEDICINE.

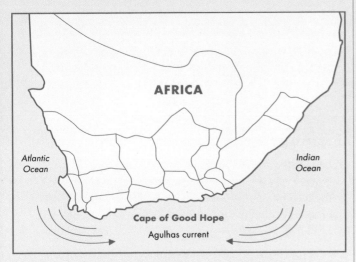

The Cape of Good Hope, a perilous area where Bartolomeu Dias recently risked sailing.

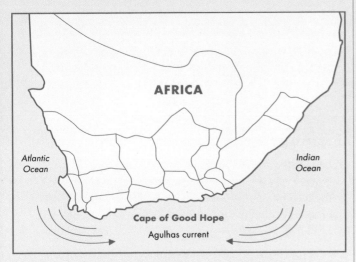

AFRICA

Atlantic Ocean

Indian Ocean

Cape of Good Hope

Agulhas current

(continued on page 2)

(continued from page 1)

treacherous waters," said Portuguese mapmaker Geo Graphias. "We had to find a away around Africa's horn."

To help sailors and navigators learn to battle the sea's harsh conditions, Prince Henry started the world's first school for sailing, navigation, and mapmaking, called the School at Sagres. As a result, future expeditions were able to venture farther along Africa's uncharted western coast. While acquiring gold and various goods from the local people, the Portuguese explorers were also the first to establish the controversial slave trade in Africa.

By the time Henry died at age 66, Portugal had reached halfway down western Africa to Cape Palmas [Sierra Leone]. Almost immediately Henry's successor, King John II, demanded more trade and additional profits. He also wanted to establish the first Portuguese settlements in Africa. After battling the native people of the land, he got his way.

In March of this year, Dias and his crew, traveling in a fleet of just two ships, reached Africa's tip, the most perilous part of the journey. Battling giant waves and heavy winds, it took the explorers 13 days to round the horn to Africa's lower east coast.

"It was a rough voyage," said crew member Lorenzo Mar. "There were times when we didn't think we'd make it through. But once we got around, the water smoothed out and we realized we had done it! We were the first to round Africa's southern tip."

In honor of the harsh conditions they faced, Dias named Africa's tip the Cape of Storms; however, there is word the king plans to change the name to the "Cape of Good Hope," in reference to the commercial importance of the new route.

The crew is expected back in Portugal in about 16 months.

The Sea Looks Swell

IN YOUR CARAVEL

Ask Mr. Map

QUESTION: Why is Portugal so desperate to round the tip of Africa?

ANSWER: For hundreds of years, the only way for traders to travel between Europe and Asia has been by way of the Silk Road, a long and winding path that stretches for miles through dangerous mountain passes and arid deserts. Travel on the Silk Road is difficult and risky, with various threats from bandits, droughts, flash floods, avalanches, heavy snow, and steep mountain passes. In contrast, traveling by sea—even over the cape's rough waters—is faster and safer.

YOUR WORLD, CHANGING WITH EVERY EXPEDITION

The Explorer's Gazette

October 13, 1492 — Volume MCDXCII No. 42 — Price: TWO GOLD FLORINS

LANDFALL!

Christopher Columbus reaches land after cross-Atlantic voyage; crew asks: "Is this China?"

GUANAHANI ISLAND, THE CARIBBEAN – Dozens of Spaniards, led by Italian navigator and explorer Christopher Columbus, descended upon the small Caribbean island of Guanahani yesterday after a nearly two-month voyage across the Atlantic Ocean.

The voyagers had originally set out to find a new route to Asia. It is unclear if that's what they've found. According to *Explorer's Gazette* sources, the new land doesn't resemble Asia at all.

"Something tells me we're not in China," said a crew member. "Columbus thinks

(continued on page 2)

The Americas—not Asia!— where Columbus just landed.

IN RECENT NEWS

Leonardo da Vinci designs "Ornithopter flying machine"; detailed drawing illustrates how man could someday use artificial wings to fly. See INNOVATIONS.

Round and round we go: Martin Behaim designs rounded map called "globe." See WORLD NEWS.

Musicians create the trombone, an instrument designed to be an improved version of the trumpet. See MUSIC.

Natives of Guanahani welcome Christopher Columbus to their shores. Columbus thinks they're Chinese.

(continued from page 1)

we've reached Asia, but I'm not so sure."

About 8 A.M. yesterday morning, Columbus and his 90-person crew, who had set out from the Spanish port of Palos on August 3, stepped onto the warm, sandy beaches of the yet unmapped island.

But the island is far from uninhabited. It is densely populated by the Taino people, who have lived there for centuries. The Taino have reportedly been friendly to Columbus and his crew, offering them food, and attempting to communicate their customs despite the language barrier.

The Taino call the island Guanahani, but Columbus has already renamed it San Salvador in honor of King Ferdinand and Queen Isabella of Spain. It was Ferdinand and Isabella who gave Columbus

Columbus plants a flag in the ground. The locals are probably wondering why.

the ships *Nina*, *Pinta*, and *Santa Maria* for the voyage.

They had hoped he would find a more direct trade route with the West Indies, a region in Asia. Columbus, an avid mapmaker and longtime navigator, has been trying to prove his theory that it is faster to get to Asia by sailing west across the Atlantic Ocean than by

sailing east. A more direct route would mean more direct trade. His theory also hinges on the idea that the world is spherical in shape, and not flat, as some Europeans still believe.

"If it's possible to sail west to reach the East, that can only mean one thing," said Spanish geographer Leonardo DeMappio, one of many to support Columbus's theories. "That the world is round."

Columbus believes he has reached his goal, that the newly named San Salvador is a part of Asia. But some fellow travelers have their doubts.

"I think we've discovered a

new country entirely," said crewman Juan Futuro. "Maybe even a new continent."

Whatever it is, the land is plentiful. According to reports, the ground is fertile and teeming with flowers and fruits, some of which have never been seen in Europe. The crew is already loading up their ships with samples of the native goods to bring back to Spain, including various spices, fruits, exotic birds, and gold. The explorers are especially excited about their discoveries of tobacco and pineapples.

Despite the Taino people's hospitality, Columbus has ordered that several of the tribesmen be brought back to Spain, likely to be sold as slaves.

Columbus and his crew are planning to return to Spain in a few months, after they visit some of the neighboring islands. According to *Explorer's Gazette* sources, more voyages are already being planned to explore the region.

"If this isn't Asia, then what is it? We've got to find out," said Portuguese mapmaker Luis Ventura. "I've got a feeling there's a lot more to discover here. A whole lot more."

ASK A STRANGER

The Taino people were reportedly friendly and hospitable to Columbus and his crew. The Explorer's Gazette *asked them: "What do you think of the explorers?"*

"They seemed very interested in our things—especially the gold. And I don't think they've ever tasted pineapple before; that seems strange."
—Yuisa, Taino chief's daughter, age 19

"They seem a little frightened by us, even though we are trying to welcome them."
—Higuamota, village medicine woman, age 45

"I don't trust them. They are taking some of our people back to their country. That's not right."
—Gueybana, Taino chief, 37

In My Crystal Ball

By Opticus, *Seer of All Things Future*

I PREDICT . . . Columbus's second voyage will bring 19 ships and 1,300 men to the Caribbean . . . By his third and fourth voyages, he'll have named most of these islands with Spanish names . . . The Taino people will be nearly extinct within 20 years . . . and American schoolchildren will love Columbus because he'll give them a school holiday.

YOUR WORLD, CHANGING WITH EVERY EXPEDITION

The Explorer's Gazette

September 30, 1513   Volume MDXIII No. 40   Price: THREE GOLD FLORINS

BALBOA BECOMES FIRST EUROPEAN TO VIEW PACIFIC OCEAN

Explorer claims all adjacent lands for Spain

Balboa and his crew take a much-needed dip in the ocean that he discovered.

PANAMA – With an endless expanse of deep blue water stretching before him and acres of thick jungles behind him, 38-year-old Spanish explorer Vasco Nuñez de Balboa last week became the first European to view the eastern edge of the Southern Sea, or Pacific Ocean.

"This was an unexpected triumph," said Hernando Explorez, one of Balboa's many followers. "When he started his journey years ago, his only intention was to find new land—and new riches."

Balboa's journey didn't begin as a quest for an ocean; it was originally a quest for gold. In 1501, he left Spain to seek the gold of Hispaniola [Haiti]. From there he headed to Columbia, where he searched for more treasures along the northern coast of South

Vasco Nuñez de Balboa

America and in the Gulf of Uraba, near San Sebastian. In Hispaniola, Balboa and his travel partner, Rodrigo de Bastidas, were forced to abandon their sinking ship. The ship had been plagued by teredo worms, which live in

tropical waters and are known to dig holes in the bottoms of wooden boats.

With no transportation or money, Balboa tried for a brief period to farm for a living. He wasn't successful.

Finally, in 1510 Balboa and his dog Leoncico were able to stow away on a boat going from Santo Domingo to San Sebastian. According to crew members who knew of the stowaways, Balboa and his dog spent the entire trip hiding in a wooden barrel.

Upon arriving in San Sebastian, Balboa convinced some of the sailors to continue on with him to Panama, to a spot he had seen in his earlier travels. There, Balboa founded

(continued on page 2)

IN RECENT NEWS

Michelangelo finishes painting the ceiling of the Sistine Chapel in Rome. See ART.

Juan Ponce de Leon discovers Florida. See WORLD NEWS.

First pineapples arrive in Europe. See FOOD & WINE.

(continued from page 1)

the first European settlement in South America, the town of Santa Maria de la Antigua del Darien.

Balboa married the daughter of the local Indian chief, and it was then that he learned about a large body of water several miles to the west. It was a sea not yet on the map, an ocean not yet named by the European explorers.

"Every explorer wants the chance to claim something for his country," said Explorez. "Balboa heard about that ocean and made it his mission to find it first."

Hundreds of Spaniards followed the native people through the thick jungles and across the Gulf of Uraba to the Darien Peninsula. After about three weeks, a native guide pointed toward a mountain. On the other side, he said, was the sea.

"At that point, Balboa wanted to do it alone," Explorez said. "He left the others at the bottom of the mountain and trudged up with his dog."

When he saw the glistening blue water, which stretched as far as the horizon, he immediately named it *Mar Del Sur*, or "Southern Sea," because he had traveled south to see it. And while Balboa claims he had the honor of setting the first European eyes on the Southern Sea, some say that's not quite the truth.

"Actually, his dog got there first," said Marco Landsendo, a crew member traveling with Balboa. "He smelled the salt water, ran up ahead of us, and barked. When we caught up with him, there it was. If Balboa wanted to be fair, he'd let the dog name the ocean."

But that's not likely to happen. Not only did Balboa name the ocean, he and his men also claimed that Spain had rights to all the land the ocean touched. According to sources, Spain is already planning future expeditions to explore the ocean and its adjacent lands.

ASK A STRANGER

Who deserves the credit for discovering the Pacific Ocean?

"A good dog always walks in front of its master. The dog."
—Fernando Fictionus, student, age 8

"How about the native people? They were living there long before the Spaniards arrived."
—Ignus Bahilla, native of Panama, age 23

"How about the fish, about a bajillion years ago?"
—Dr. Jasper Cutreilly, scientist, age 48

"It should be called the Amoeba Ocean. They were there first."
—Edward San Sebastian, marine biologist and historian, age 55

How to Hide in a Barrel

1. Get a barrel.
2. Make sure it's empty, and not full of wine or nails.
3. Drill little holes in the sides for air. (Important!)
4. Pack more food and water than you think you'll need.
5. If traveling with a dog, bring little treats and a clothespin for your nose. (Very important!)
6. Address the barrel to your destination. Be sure to use the correct postage.
7. Get in and pull the lid shut tight.
8. Get out, call the delivery service, then get back in again.
9. Wait.
10. Get out when your recipient says, "You can get out now."
11. Shower. (Extremely important!)

Warning to Sailors!

Don't let pirates write copies of your maps. Protect copyrights! Piracy is theft.

A public service message from the Mapmaker's Guild.

In My Crystal Ball

By Opticus, *Seer of All Things Future*

I PREDICT . . . the discovery of the Southern Sea, albeit disputed, will be the high point of Balboa's career . . . Six years from now, in 1519, Balboa will lose his head . . . literally lose it . . . And what's worse, the explorer Magellan will soon rename Balboa's ocean *Mar Pacifica* [Pacific Ocean], meaning "peaceful sea."

YOUR WORLD, CHANGING WITH EVERY EXPEDITION

The Explorer's Gazette

August 14, 1521   Volume MDXXI No. 33   Price: THREE GOLD FLORINS

CORTEZ'S VICTORY IS THE AZTECS' DEFEAT

Empire falls, Mexico renamed "New Spain"

TENOCHTITLÁN, "NEW SPAIN" – After a historic battle that ended with the loss of more than 120,000 Aztecs and the destruction of the capital city of Tenochtitlán, Mexico, Spanish conquistador Hernando Cortez has successfully overthrown the Aztec empire and claimed Mexico for Spain.

Cortez, who has already elected himself governor of the land, renamed the country "New Spain."

"Our armies were no match for theirs," said surviving Tenochtitlán resident Juahar Chazo. "We don't have the guns, the swords, or the horses

that they do. We were at a disadvantage."

The victory was reportedly no surprise to Cortez, who has gained a reputation as a determined and merciless leader.

Since his boyhood in Medellin, Spain, Cortez has been a steadfast soldier. He joined the Spanish military at age 18, and helped General Velásquez conquer Cuba in 1511. Velásquez rewarded him by appointing him mayor of Cuba.

A few years later he got restless. In 1518, Cortez stole eleven of Velásquez's ships and set sail for Mexico with a crew of 500 men. After short stops in

Locals watch Hernando Cortez as he and his crew enter Mexico. They actually believe he is a god.

In a bold move, Cortez decides to keep his crew from leaving Mexico by sinking most of the ships.

Yucatan, Cortez and his crew landed near Veracruz, where the local Cempoala people greeted him with gifts of food, feathers, and gold. Soon after that, ambassadors from the Aztec emperor Moctezuma II (Montezuma) arrived with additional gifts.

"They were friendly to us because they mistook us for gods," said crewman Gabriel Juarez, who added that they were the ones who brought the first 16 horses into North America. "I think it was our

(continued on page 2)

IN RECENT NEWS

Explorer Ferdinand Magellan reaches the Philippines. See WORLD NEWS.

Wealthy Europeans love newly invented "pocket watch"; inventor Peter Henlein talks about how it works. See INNOVATIONS.

Explorer's Gazette interview: Michelangelo talks about his work at the Sistine Chapel. See ART.

(continued from page 1)

horses. They had never seen horses before."

It became clear that the natives were befriending Cortez because they mistook him for the legendary Quetzalcoatl, a mythical man-god who was predicted to return to one day to Mexico. Cortez didn't bother correcting them.

Cortez kneels before Moctezuma (Montezuma). Later, he's not so polite.

"He liked the people thinking he was a god," Juarez said. "It certainly made it easier to explore and plunder the land."

Cortez had heard there was gold deep in the jungle, off the coast. To discourage his crewmen from retreating, he burned all of his ships except one and set off in search of Mexico's riches. A few months later, he and his men reached the city of Tenochtitlán, the capital of Mexico.

Still under the impression that Cortez was a god, Moctezuma welcomed him and his men, giving them gifts of food and gold, and allowing them to stay in his father's palace.

But Cortez wanted more. He made Moctezuma promise to send shipments of gold to Spain every year for as long as he lived. He also asked that the Aztecs construct shrines to the Virgin Mary in their

Pros and Cons

He may be a wealthy landowner, but he's not a nice guy!

An editorial by Chaz Aztec

Fellow Mexicans! Look at Cortez . . . he has destroyed a timeless civilization. He has made slaves of thousands of us Aztecs and killed thousands more. He pretends to conquer in the name of spreading religion, but he makes himself the wealthiest guy in town. If he attempts any more expeditions, let's ask our gods to wreck his ships in terrible storms. It's the least we can do.

temples. All of his demands were met.

Despite the hospitality, Cortez took Moctezuma hostage and tried to govern the city through him. The Aztecs revolted, and Moctezuma was killed during an uprising.

United in their anger, the Aztecs were initially able to drive the Spaniards out of the city—but not for long. Less

than a year later, Cortez returned with a bigger army. This time, the Aztec military was no match for the Spaniards' more advanced weaponry.

After a fierce battle that destroyed almost the entire city and killed between 120,000 and 200,000 Aztecs, the new Aztec emperor, Cuauhtémoc, surrendered.

In My Crystal Ball

By Opticus, *Seer of All Things Future*

I PREDICT . . . Cortez is too itchy for power to live quietly . . . He will pay to lead an expedition to southern California and finance many others . . . His men will hate him . . . His ships will be wrecked in terrible storms . . . He will go broke . . . He will return to Spain a wreck of a man . . . He will set sail for Mexico in 1547, but land in Andalusia, Spain, near death . . . He will die in his sleep at the age of 62 . . . His body will be moved to Mexico . . . where not a single monument will be erected to him for at least 450 years.

ASK MR. MAP

QUESTION: Who are the Aztecs?

ANSWER: Until recently, the Aztecs have ruled most of Mexico. They built several great cities including Tenochtitlán. It had a royal palace and many temples. The great city—and empire—has now fallen. An Aztec poet just wrote the following about his people's misfortune:

How can we save our homes, my people
The Aztecs are deserting the city
The city is in flames and all
is darkness and destruction
Weep my people
Know that with these disasters
We have lost the Mexican nation
The water has turned bitter
Our food is bitter
These are the acts of the Giver of Life.

YOUR WORLD, CHANGING WITH EVERY EXPEDITION

The Explorer's Gazette

September 7, 1522   Volume MDXXII No. 37   Price: THREE GOLD FLORINS

BITTERSWEET VICTORY:
MAGELLAN'S AROUND-THE-WORLD VOYAGE COMPLETED WITHOUT HIM

Only 18 men return from historic mission; lead explorer killed during journey

Magellan on the bow of his ship surveying the land ahead.

SEVILLE, SPAIN – It was a mission filled with misfortune. A mission that started out with almost 300 men and ended with just 18, that began with five ships and ended with just one. But it was a mission that was successful.

Yesterday the remaining 18 men of Ferdinand Magellan's around-the-world voyage arrived in Spain, their historic mission finished after three years at sea. Unfortunately, the Portuguese-born Magellan wasn't there to accept the honors, having died two years into the journey.

"He died for what he lived for," said aspiring explorer Pedro Oceanez. "At least some of his men made it."

Magellan's five ships, *Trinidad, Concepción, San Antonio, Santiago,* and *Victoria,* left Spain on Sept. 20, 1519, headed on a new westward route toward Southeast Asia. It was a controversial course, since most sailors go east around India to reach Asia.

Magellan, who knew the experimental route would cause conflict, didn't tell his crew about his westward plan. Nevertheless, mutiny erupted when the crew realized they were sailing on an unfamiliar route.

"They didn't know where they were going," said navigator Antonio Wave. "They didn't want to sail a route that hadn't already been mapped. Some of them still believed the Earth was flat, and you'd fall off if you went too far. But mostly, it was the fear of the unknown that scared them."

Though Magellan's angry crew was eventually calmed, there were other problems. After its initial Atlantic crossing, the *Santiago* sunk in a storm when Magellan ordered

(continued on page 2)

IN RECENT NEWS

Leonardo da Vinci, painter of the *Mona Lisa,* dies in Italy. See ARTS.

Chocolate arrives in Spain; royal family says "Delicioso!" See FOOD.

Hernando Cortez continues conquest of Mexico; thousands of natives defeated. See WORLD NEWS.

The newly discovered Strait of Magellan, which the explorer decided to name after himself.

vive the voyage, his navigational skills were crucial in getting the ships through the uncharted waters of the earth.

"Really, Magellan's biggest feat was venturing into the unknown," Oceanez said. "Nobody had ever sailed that far, but he wasn't afraid."

Magellan was very nearly the first to circle the Earth.

(continued from page 1)

its crew to sail ahead and find a safe passage around Patagonia. The fleet lost another ship when the crew of the *San Antonio* retreated back to Spain with much of the fleet's food.

In a brief stroke of luck, the fleet discovered a 373-mile (597 meters) shortcut through the tip of South America, a water passage that they named the Strait of Magellan.

After that, it was far from smooth sailing. Crossing the Pacific Ocean, which Magellan named to mean "Peaceful Sea," took longer than expected. No land was sighted for nearly two months.

Desperate, the men were forced to eat all that was left on the ships, including rats and leather straps. The ship's fresh water supply was contaminated—it turned yellow!—and dozens of men died from scurvy, an illness caused by a lack of Vitamin C.

By the time Magellan's fleet reached the Philippines in March of 1521, only 115 of his crewmen were left.

Then, on April 27, almost two years after starting his around-the-world journey, Magellan himself was killed while fighting in a native uprising in the Philippines. The crew sailed on, determined to finish what Magellan had started.

But misfortunes continued. Shortly after leaving the Philippines, the *Concepción* was deemed unseaworthy and abandoned. The remaining two ships went on to Borneo and the Moluccas, where they loaded the decks with spices. Then the *Trinidad* was wrecked on its way to Panama.

With thousands of miles left to travel, the *Victoria*, commanded by Juan Sebastián del Cano, was their last hope.

After sailing across the Indian Ocean, rounding the Cape of Good Hope, and heading north along the coast of Africa, the ship reached Seville.

While Magellan didn't sur-

In My Crystal Ball

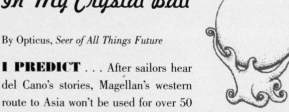

By Opticus, *Seer of All Things Future*

I PREDICT . . . After sailors hear del Cano's stories, Magellan's western route to Asia won't be used for over 50 years . . . the voyage will give science the first real proof the earth is round . . . it will reveal the Americas as a new world separate from Asia . . . and explorers won't attempt to rename the Pacific Ocean when the name finally catches on.

ASK ESTHER,
the Mediterranean Chef

Dear Esther,
Why are so many people traveling long distances for spices?
—The Original Spice Girl

Dear O.S.G.,
There are so many exciting modern uses for spices. Since spices come from plants, they're light and easy to transport. Traders treat spices just like money. No wonder Asia is now crawling with explorers—spices can make you very, very rich! Here's why:

Food rots!
Since there's no such thing as a refrigerator, salt helps preserve meats longer. Other spices help hide the taste of spoiled food.

We smell bad!
Polite people take baths every few months. In between, spices hide our natural pungencies. We put spices in soaps and perfumes. Perfumed candles also keep your home from smelling like your pigsty.

We get sick!
Spices and herbs make good medicines. Today's modern, sixteenth-century doctors say that nutmeg cures most cancers and cinnamon cures the common cold. And whether or not cloves make the blood thicker, they sure make ham taste great.

Spices are the spice of life!
—Esther

Your World, Changing with Every Expedition

The Explorer's Gazette

May 22, 1542   Volume MDXLII No. 21   Price: THREE GOLD FLORINS

NO GOLD AT END OF THE RAINBOW FOR DE SOTO

After long treasure hunt across New World, explorer dies empty-handed

MISSISSIPPI RIVER, NEW WORLD – The grand, treasure-seeking adventures of another Spanish explorer have officially hit a dead end.

Hernando De Soto, the first European to explore Florida, died yesterday after four years of scouring the warm southern region of the New World and finding none of the treasures he was seeking.

"He might not have found any gold or silver, but at least he found Florida," said Spanish historian Francis Boone. "His observations and descriptions of the land will fuel many more expeditions to the New World."

From the very start, De Soto was an ambitious leader. At the age of 14 he sailed to Panama and became the local governor's aide. A few years later he began a 10-year exploration of Central America, continually growing in stature the more he strove onward.

In 1530 De Soto joined the

Hernando De Soto on his boat as it heads toward the Mississippi River.

crew of notorious conquistador Francisco Pizarro, known for his explorations of Peru as well as his violent conquering of its native people. In less than a year, Pizarro and his crew overtook and destroyed Peru's Incan empire.

After helping Pizarro conquer the Incas, De Soto filled his trunk with hundreds of pounds of gold and fled back to Spain a very wealthy man. Upon returning, he got married and bought a mansion to begin

a new life as a family man.

But he didn't stay long. In 1536 Charles, King of Spain, gave De Soto the chance to be governor of Florida and Cuba. To do so, he would have to leave Spain and return to the New World, where the region would have to be converted into colonies. De Soto accepted the challenge.

Convinced that Florida was rich with gold and other treasures, De Soto raised a crew and set sail. His fleet of nine ships,

IN RECENT NEWS

Going West: Spanish Explorers arrive in California after long trek across country. See NEW LANDS.

Europeans getting used to new "flush" toilets; makes bathrooms a lot less messy. See INVENTIONS.

Copernicus, a Polish astronomer and mathematician, set to publish theory that Earth and the other planets revolve around the Sun. See WORLD NEWS.

Enough Already! Henry VIII marries sixth wife. See POLITICS.

including the massive *San Christoval*, reached Havana, Cuba, in 1538. In May of 1539, they crossed the Gulf of Mexico to Florida.

(continued on page 2)

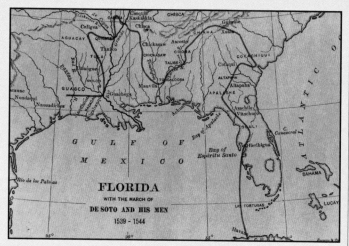

De Soto's route across the southern part of the continent. He journeyed across much of this area in search of gold.

(continued from page 1)

On May 30, 1539, De Soto pulled up to the west coast of Florida with more than 600 soldiers, priests, and explorers in tow. The men spent nearly four years searching for gold, silver, and jewels, while exploring the area and brutally conquering native tribes, including the Cherokees, Seminoles, Creeks, Appalachians, and Choctaws.

"It's like a war there, between the natives and the Europeans," said a crew member. "They're angry we're taking their land away. But we keep taking it."

Explorer's Gazette sources described the region in and around Florida as a dense marshland with a warm, humid climate. The soil is rich with vegetation and fertile for farming.

After exploring Florida, De Soto and his crew trudged nearly halfway across the continent in search of gold. They trekked through Georgia, the Carolinas, into Tennessee, and through Alabama. They were the first Europeans to cross the Mississippi River and journey up the Arkansas River into Oklahoma.

Finally, after four long years of exploration, De Soto contracted a fever and died. His crewmates plan on hiding his

De Soto and his men meet the Native Americans on their tour of discovery. He conquered many of the tribes he met.

body inside a hollow tree and then throwing it into the Mississippi River so that the natives, whom he had violently mistreated while colonizing the region, will not learn of his death.

"Maybe it was just too much disappointment for him," said Di Nero. "There was all this land to explore, but we never found any of the things he was seeking. We never found any treasure."

EXPLORER'S MAZE:
Can you find the GOLD?

De Soto didn't have any luck finding treasure in the New World. See if you can do better than he did, or if you too will end up in the Mississippi River.

Your World, Changing with Every Expedition

 # The Explorer's Gazette

April 5, 1581   Volume MDLXXXI No. 15   Price: THREE GOLD FLORINS

WHAT A DAY FOR A KNIGHT!

Sir Francis Drake knighted for his "profitable explorations"; queen overlooks piracy, slavery

Francis Drake

PLYMOUTH, ENGLAND – Francis Drake has made powerful enemies—and powerful friends.

A British explorer, slave trader, pirate, and naval officer, Drake has sailed around the world and fought wars at home. He has sunken ships and robbed settlements. He has angered Spain and filled England's treasury with thousands of dollars in stolen loot.

And now he has become a knight. Queen Elizabeth passed down the honor yesterday, shortly after Drake arrived back from his latest around-the-world journey.

"This is a big deal for a man of humble origins," said London professor Bartleby Mattison. "He went from vagabond to royalty in one day. What an amazing accomplishment!"

It's a big step up for Drake, who grew up poor, living on a rickety boat with his family. When he was 13, instead of getting married, as many boys did at that age, Drake took to the seas, seeking adventure.

Around the age of 20 Drake became a privateer, which meant he was a pirate working for the government, authorized during wartime to attack and capture enemy vessels.

In the 1560s, the devoutly religious Drake was one of the first to bring African slaves to the Caribbean. He sold his human cargo to the Spanish, often robbing their ships before heading home.

In 1573 Drake orchestrated the "Great Silver Train Robbery," leading a crew of French privateers and Cimaroons (African slaves who had escaped the Spanish) on the heist, which netted him a fortune in Spanish gold.

Meanwhile, the queen, who had sponsored his raids, couldn't publicly acknowledge the robbery since she had signed a truce with Spain; however, she was impressed, and

IN RECENT NEWS

World population surpasses 500 million; enough already! See WORLD NEWS.

Modern calendar introduced by Pope Gregory XIII; "leap year" requires leap of faith. See CALENDAR.

English Parliament outlaws Roman Catholicism, keeps the calendar. See POLITICS.

---

secretly rewarded him with a portion of the gold.

Drake's biggest accomplishment came in 1577, when he made the second-ever voyage around the world. Portuguese explorer Ferdinand Magellan had led the first voyage, but he died toward the end of the long journey.

"No wonder the trip killed Magellan," said Churchill Tripper, a crewman on one of Drake's five ships. "It took us three years."

Along the journey, Drake and his crew were busy. They

After raiding their homes, Drake boards local residents on his ship.

(continued on page 2)

ASK A STRANGER

How will the queen's acceptance of pirates change your life?

"We'll have to let their parrots keep interrupting for crackers."
—Wharton Williams, fisherman, age 59

"When a pirate wants to shake my hand with his hook, do I have to?"
—Guinevere McFadden, seamstress, age 29

"Excellent. I'm going to the bathtub to steal my brother's boat."
—Priscilla Periwinkle, preschooler, age 4

(continued from page 1)

robbed Spanish ships and raided settlements in Panama, Chile, and Peru. Drake also claimed a part of Northern California for the queen, and explored the western coast of North America; reportedly he went as far north as Vancouver, Canada.

The voyage also had its share of discoveries. Drake and his crew were the first to determine that South America isn't connected to Antarctica. And they were the first to sail to the location where the Atlantic and Pacific Oceans meet.

"And we found a lot of gold," Tripper exclaimed. "A whole world full of gold."

By the end of the three-year journey, only 58 of the original 166 English returned to England.

In My Crystal Ball

By Opticus, *Seer of All Things Future*

I PREDICT . . . In 1587, the Queen will send Drake to help win an unavoidable war with Spain . . . In 1588, Drake will destroy the powerful Spanish fleet in Cádiz, Spain . . . He will be promoted to vice admiral . . . He will return to serve in England's Parliament . . . In 1595, the Queen will dust off Drake and send him to the Caribbean to fight even more Spanish soldiers . . . The mission will fail and, even worse, Drake will die there of dysentery, only to be buried at sea among the ships he sank.

How to Recognize a Pirate Ship

By Professor Benjamin Bundt

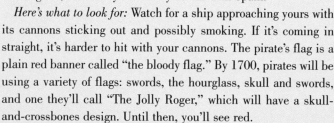

As the Spanish know, pirates are most common in the Mediterranean and Caribbean Seas. Usually they attack those plump Spanish ships transporting huge loads of gold back from Mexico and South America. The most notable pirates are English, since they're usually at war with Spain.

Here's what to look for: Watch for a ship approaching yours with its cannons sticking out and possibly smoking. If it's coming in straight, it's harder to hit with your cannons. The pirate's flag is a plain red banner called "the bloody flag." By 1700, pirates will be using a variety of flags: swords, the hourglass, skull and swords, and one they'll call "The Jolly Roger," which will have a skull-and-crossbones design. Until then, you'll see red.

Drake and his peers are called "privateers" because they attack enemy ships for their country. They make out like bandits. Regular pirates don't. Most die early, since doctors avoid pirate ships. Pirates also get arrested, or get blown to bits by ships they underestimate. Unlucky pirates are often left stranded on remote islands and aren't welcome in established ports. Lucky ones get treasure, bury it, and lose the map in a poker game. For fun, these fellows enjoy drinking, robbing their friends, and mutiny.

"¡Imposible!" says Spanish king

By Xerxes Hammond

MADRID – The Most Royal King Phillip II of Spain announces that he is not amused by Drake's British knighthood. Here in Spain, Drake is called "El Draque" (the Dragon), because he is a thief, a crook, a pirate, and a bad guy. "¡Qué terible!" said the King. "¡El Draque es un criminal!" The King went on and on about stolen gold, sunken ships, and land disputes.

Your World, Changing with Every Expedition

The Explorer's Gazette

April 1, 1611   Volume MDCXI No. 14   Price: THREE GOLD FLORINS

ABANDONED! HENRY HUDSON'S CREW REVOLTS

Explorer sent up his own river without a paddle

Above: Henry Hudson is traveling light, but not by choice. Left: Hudson looking scruffy (and cold!) during a long voyage.

Henry Hudson as a young man.

HUDSON BAY, CANADA – Henry Hudson, the man who led four expeditions in search of a sea route to Asia and instead became the first explorer to navigate the Hudson River, was recently abandoned by his crew in the bay that bears his name.

The angry sailors reportedly left the navigator floating in a small boat in the bay after a mutiny that began when Hudson demanded they stay and explore the region. The crewmembers, who had already endured a cold, hunger-filled winter there, decided that enough was enough.

"We couldn't take it anymore," said one of the sailors. "We'd been shivering and starving there for more than a year."

The fateful expedition departed from England in 1610. Hudson had set out to find the Northwest Passage, the waterbound route linking Europe with Asia that would make trade between the two regions easier.

They never got there, though. Instead, traveling between Greenland and Labrador, Hudson sailed through the Hudson Strait and into the Hudson Bay. It wasn't the Northwest Passage, but it was something.

The journey marked the fourth time that Hudson failed to find the route to Asia while making an alternate discovery in its place. On his first voyage in 1607, Hudson set out on his ship the *Hopewell* to locate a passage to the East through the Arctic Ocean by way of the North Pole. He was stopped by icy waters 577 miles (923 km) from the pole and never found it. His second voyage met a similarly chilly fate.

In 1609 he was hired to take the *Half Moon* on the same cold voyage. After reaching Greenland he realized once again he wasn't going to find a route to Asia, so he decided

against orders to sail west toward North America.

"He couldn't return to England without finding *something*," observed London

(continued on page 2)

IN RECENT NEWS

Dutch invent refracting telescope, point it at the Americas. See INNOVATIONS.

Galileo publishes research on planets, rocks the world. See OUTER SPACE NEWS.

King James likes new version of Bible enough to name it after himself. See RELIGION.

(continued from page 1)

university professor Winston Bookbinder.

With 20 Dutch and English sailors on board, Hudson explored North America's eastern coast from Maine to North Carolina. They were the first Europeans to describe the areas that would later become Maine, Cape Cod, and Manhattan (although Giovanni de Verrazano explored the same coast in 1524). They also sailed the New York Harbor and were the first to head north toward Albany on the river now named after Hudson.

"He didn't fail entirely," said British geographer Henry Trumpet. "He may not have found the Northwest Passage, but he brought back a wealth of knowledge about the east coast."

On Hudson's last voyage in 1610, he went much farther, taking his ship, *The Discovery*, through Canada's Hudson Straight to the Hudson Bay. The crew had intended to return home after exploring and mapping the Hudson Bay region for several months, but their ship was frozen in the icy cold waters of the bay, and they were forced to spend the winter there.

It was a rough winter, with little food and water. By March the crew had been reduced to eating frogs and moss. Regardless, Hudson wanted to stay and continue exploring. His crew didn't like that idea.

Starving and diseased, they revolted, leaving Hudson, his son, and seven of his loyal crewmen adrift in the bay in a small boat.

"Without food or water, it's not likely they'll survive," said crewman Miles Swindler. "My guess is they won't see another winter."

Hudson's ship the *Half Moon* in New York Harbor before the mutiny.

In My Crystal Ball

By Opticus, *Seer of All Things Future*

I PREDICT . . . After being abandoned by his crew in the Hudson Bay, Henry Hudson will never be seen again . . . Captain Hudson's harbor observations will interest his old bosses, the Dutch East India Company . . . In 1624 they will set up a colony there called New Amsterdam . . . The British will ultimately name it New York.

Holiday History
All the World Is Fool for a Day!

By Cort Jesters

Today is April Fool's Day, a holiday celebrated by carrying out practical jokes and hoaxes in the name of bringing great embarrassment to friends and family alike.

How did it start? The holiday was believed to originate in 1582, when the Gregorian calendar replaced the old Julian calendar. With the new calendar, the New Year was moved from April 1 to January 1. But some people either refused to accept the new New Year or didn't know about the change. As a joke, others would send them funny gifts or invitations to nonexistent New Year's parties.

Remember: If you plan on playing a prank, do it before noon! Jokes played after 12:00 P.M. are rumored to bring bad luck to the jokester.

Your World, Changing with Every Expedition

The Explorer's Gazette

June 16, 1643   Volume MDCXLIII No. 25   Price: THREE GOLD FLORINS

ABEL TASMAN EXPLORES DOWN UNDER

New lands, new faces: "Tasmanian devil" named after first European to reach southern Australia

Abel Tasman

VAN DIEMEN'S LAND, AUSTRALIA – Some explorers get countries, rivers, or islands named in their honor; Abel Tasman, the first European to explore the islands off the southern coast of Australia, got more than that.

He got a ferocious little carnivore to take his name.

The "Tasmanian devil," as the strange creature will now be known, was named in honor of Tasman's recent explorations of Australia and its neighboring lands.

"The discovery of this animal is almost as exciting as the discovery of the land itself," said Amsterdam-based zoologist Harvey Wild. "Tasman should be proud of all his findings, the living, breathing ones as well as the ones that are surrounded by oceans."

Tasman, a Dutch navigator, was assigned by the Dutch East India Company (DEIC) to explore new trade routes throughout the Australian region. He encountered the animal during his recent travel through an island he called Van Diemen's Land; sources say that land will be renamed "Tasmania," also in honor of Tasman.

The journey began on August 13, 1642, when 40-year-old

IN RECENT NEWS

Louis XIV is crowned King of France at age 4. See POLITICS.

Colony of New Sweden is established. See WORLD NEWS.

Evangelista Torricelli invents mercury barometer; instrument to be used to measure atmospheric pressure. See INNOVATIONS.

Tasman, in command of two ships and about 110 men, set sail from the port of Batavia, Indonesia. Four months later, his crew spotted land.

According to navigators, Tasmania sits about 150 miles (240 km) south of the Australian mainland and is a lush island with varying terrains ranging from mountains and lakes to rivers and rain forests. It is also reportedly teeming with wildlife never before seen in Europe.

"Some of these animals carry their young in pouches built into their stomachs," said Wild.

(continued on page 2)

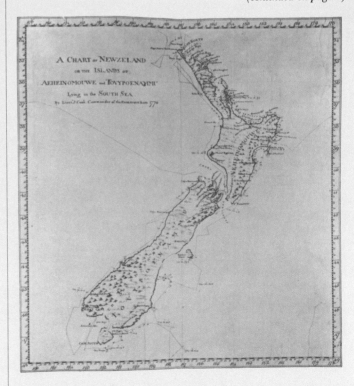

Tasman is excited that he found New Zealand. The same can't be said of the natives.

(continued from page 1)

"I've never heard of anything like it. And that Tasmanian devil—he sure is a mean one," Wild added.

Biologists believe that the Tasmanian devil, a relatively small animal best described as a cross between a pig and a dog, can only be found in this part of the world. Primarily a scavenger that feeds on dead carcasses, it is prone to baring its sharp teeth and letting out loud, intimidating growls.

But Tasman's intentions weren't to discover new animals. As a part of his 10-year contract with the DEIC, he had been instructed to search for the elusive "Southern Continent" that supposedly stretches across the Pacific. And while he may not have found the entire continent, he did explore dozens of islands near the southern tip of Australia.

Another significant discovery was that of "Staten Landt," the Land of the [Dutch] States. That region, far bigger than Tasmania but not nearly as large as Australia, will reportedly be renamed "New Zealand" after the Dutch province Zeelandt.

Claiming the new land wasn't easy. When Tasman's men tried to come ashore, they were met by the native Maori people. According to *Explorer's Gazette* sources, tribesmen paddled toward the sailors in canoes and sunk a small Dutch boat before approaching the larger ships. In opposition, the Dutch shot and killed a Maori man. Tasman chose to name the site "Murderer's Bay."

On June 15, Tasman returned to the port of Batavia by way of Fiji and New Guinea. On his next mission, Tasman will reportedly explore the northern region of Australia.

Field Guide to
Tasmanian Devils

With guest expert Professor Harry N. Fast

THE TASMANIAN DEVIL (*Sarcophilus harrisii*) is a carnivorous marsupial. It is found exclusively on Tasmania. It's the size of a strong little lamb, is usually black, can screech very loudly, and smells awful. It eats small animals, preferably if they're already dead.

In My Crystal Ball

By Opticus, *Seer of All Things Future*

I PREDICT . . . Tasman will do a bit more exploring, but nothing significant . . . He'll play pirate but fail to rob a Spanish ship of its treasure . . . A drunken Captain Tasman will try tough love on two disobedient sailors and personally attempt to hang them . . . He'll bungle it and lose his job for a year . . . He'll die in 1659 after mapping substantial portions of Australia.

Navigating South of the Equator

By Monocle Tati

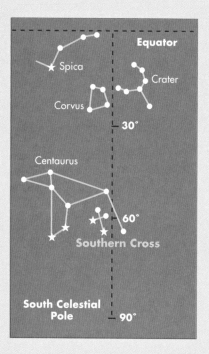

Feeling lost in Australia? Can't find your way in Fiji? Don't try to look for the North Star to find your way home.

In the Southern Hemisphere (the part of the Earth's surface that is south of the equator, including Africa, Australia, South America and Antarctica), sailors use the Southern Cross, which points south, to navigate their way across the ocean.

To find it: Locate a dark patch in the Milky Way, a band of millions of faraway stars. On one side is the Southern Cross, a constellation of four stars in the shape of a Christian cross. It is situated above the South Pole in the Antarctic Circle, making it easy to see when sailing south.

The Explorer's Gazette

DECEMBER 19, 1741   **VOLUME MDCCXLI No. 51**   **PRICE: FOUR GOLD FLORINS**

ALASKA AND RUSSIA DIVIDED BY WATERWAY!

Vitus Bering discovers "Bering Strait" during icy expedition

BERING SEA, RUSSIA – On the latest of his many journeys through the Arctic region, Vitus Bering, a navigator and captain of the Russian Navy, recently proved that Russia and Alaska are not connected by land, as was previously thought.

According to Bering's maps, the two lands are separated by a 53-mile (85-km) stretch of water, soon to be named the Bering Strait in honor of the brave explorer.

"All this time, Russians have

Vitus Bering

thought the two lands were connected," said Russian geographer Franken Trudgnik. "Now it's clear they're not."

(continued on page 2)

IN RECENT NEWS

Bavarians love counting the minutes with new "cuckoo clock." See INNOVATIONS.

Ben Franklin invents wood-burning stove; item a hot seller in America. See FOOD AND DINING.

First textile mills open in England; Industrial Revolution begins. See TECHNOLOGY.

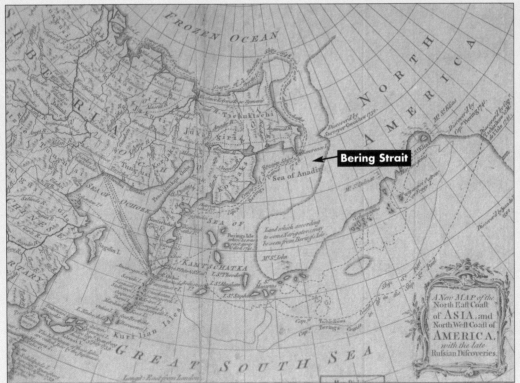

Bering Strait

Vitus Bering's discovery of this strip of water shows, once and for all, that Russia and Alaska are not connected by land.

(continued from page 1)

Vitus Jonassen Bering was born in Denmark in 1681. He spent most of his life as a sailor, navigator, mapmaker, and explorer, and was known for being a fair and balanced leader.

In 1725, after leading many expeditions and military missions through Russia's cold and uncharted waters, he was chosen by Russian Czar Peter I to explore the farthest reaches of Siberia. Bering did as he was told, leading a large crew over 5,000 miles (8,000 km).

The journeys were difficult, often through subzero temperatures and dangerously cold waters. Scurvy, an often fatal illness caused by a lack of Vitamin C, was a common affliction among crew members, since fresh fruits and vegetables were hard to come by on the long, cold voyages. On one mission, Bering lost five of his own children due to the harsh conditions.

But misfortune did not deter him. In 1728 he sailed north through what would later be known as the Bering Straight but, sighting no land, did not realize its importance.

"He actually discovered the Bering Strait long before he knew it," said one crewmate Vladimir Explornikov. "If he had only known what a great discovery he had made, maybe he would have retired earlier."

He returned to St. Petersburg in 1730. Shortly afterward he oversaw the exploration and mapping of much of Siberia.

Then, in 1741, he set out toward Alaska with two ships, the *St. Peter* and *St. Paul*, in his fleet. Somewhere in the Bering Sea, the vessels were separated, and on July 16 Bering sighted the St. Elias Mountains in Alaska. He had discovered the strait for the second time.

"He didn't realize he had almost gotten to that same point years before," Explornikov said. "But there it was. It was a victory."

It is thought that the Bering Strait was once a land bridge between the easternmost parts of Russia and Alaska, but that the seas overflowed it about 10,000 years ago, at the end of the Ice Age. The land bridge, while it existed, likely allowed the migration of settlers from Asia into the Americas about 12,000 years ago.

While Bering and his crew claimed Alaska for Russia, it is likely to one day be purchased by the Americas, the land to which it is joined.

Where Now, Sea Cow?

By Salty C. Rancher

Naturalist Wilhelm Steller was along with Bering for the ride. His studies of natural history describe both plants and animals in the Bering Sea. He is the first to discover—and the only naturalist to study—the Steller sea cow, a rare sea lion relative that is easy to catch and tastes like beef. Steller's account of the sea cow will no doubt inspire others to taste them, too.

ASK A STRANGER

Russia and Alaska aren't connected. How will that affect you?

"I will have to stop mushing when I reach the Siberian coast."
—Bob Tracker, sled-dog racer, age 37

"I'd like to go back and forth on a boat some day."
—Miriam Modelle, contessa, age 25

"Uh-oh. I smell tourists."
—Herb, seal, age 6 (in seal years)

In My Crystal Ball

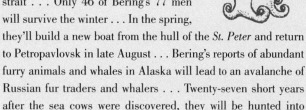

By Opticus, *Seer of All Things Future*

I PREDICT . . . Bering will die of scurvy shortly after his discovery of the strait . . . Only 46 of Bering's 77 men will survive the winter . . . In the spring, they'll build a new boat from the hull of the *St. Peter* and return to Petropavlovsk in late August . . . Bering's reports of abundant furry animals and whales in Alaska will lead to an avalanche of Russian fur traders and whalers . . . Twenty-seven short years after the sea cows were discovered, they will be hunted into extinction . . . In 1867, Russia will sell Alaska to the U.S.A. for $7.2 million, or two cents an acre.

Ask Mr. Map

QUESTION: Is a strait always straight?

ANSWER: Most definitely not. Just look at the maps of the Strait of Magellan (Issue 37) and Bering Strait if you don't believe me. A strait is a narrow passageway connecting two large bodies of water. Straits are shortcuts for ships, and this makes them important. Once they are discovered, they become busy routes used to ship goods around the world.

The Explorer's Gazette

FEBRUARY 14, 1778 **VOLUME MDCCLXXVIII No. 7** **PRICE: FOUR GOLD FLORINS**

JAMES COOK DISCOVERS HAWAIIAN ISLANDS

Voyage caps a decade of exploration

Captain James Cook

THE SANDWICH ISLANDS [HAWAII] – Captain James Cook, one of England's most highly regarded navigators, has done it again.

Cook, the first European to map a large portion of Australia, recently announced his discovery of the Hawaiian Islands, a lush, tropical cluster of islands in the Pacific Ocean. The most recent voyage marks nearly 100,000 miles (160,000 km) at sea for the accomplished sailor.

But that's not surprising. Cook has been navigating the sea since he was kid. He became a sailor at the age of 18 and a Royal Marine Captain at 29. Since then he has built a reputation as a highly skilled navigator and mapmaker, fearless in his explorations of the Southern Hemisphere.

He began his expeditions in 1768, when he was ordered to set up an observatory in Tahiti to chart the movement of the

Cook and some of his crew meet the locals of the Hawaiian Islands.

planet Venus in the night sky.

From there, he explored the South Pacific in search of the mythical continent of Terra Australis, which was believed to be a large land mass stretching across the entire hemisphere. Cook expressed doubts about its existence, but followed his orders. By circling the continent of New Zealand and mapping its coastline, he proved that the concept of Terra Australis was impossible.

"If you can sail all the way around New Zealand it means that New Zealand isn't connected to any other continent," said British navigator Herman Trust. "Most likely, the Southern Hemisphere is made up of many different lands."

It seems so. Cook went on to Australia, where he discovered its eastern coast and also made extensive maps of the coastline and several islands in the vicinity.

In 1772 he braved the icy conditions of Antarctica, zigzagging the glaciers and icebergs in an effort to make an accurate map of the land and its surrounding waters. It was a rough journey, with his crewmen battling dangerous conditions and frigid temperatures, but Cook soldiered on, jotting down observations for his navigational charts.

"Before you can have a map, you need a mapmaker," said British geographer Harry West. "Cook is one of the best."

Indeed, Cook is famous for his thorough planning and

(continued on page 2)

IN RECENT NEWS

New World colonists talk about life after signing of Declaration of Independence. See OPINION.

Benjamin Franklin reportedly developing bifocal eyeglasses for easier reading. See INNOVATIONS.

Book Review: Encyclopedia Britannica (second edition). See LITERATURE.

The natives are upset that strangers are on their land and fighting has erupted.

(continued from page 1)

superb mapmaking abilities. He is also hailed for his revolutionary use of lemons to keep his sailors free of scurvy. Scurvy, caused by a lack of Vitamin C, is a common affliction among men at sea, who do not have access to fresh fruits and vegetables during long journeys.

On July 12, 1776, Cook left on his most recent expedition. His goal was to reach the Northwest Passage, a mythical and mysterious waterway connecting the oceans through Canada.

He never found it, though many educated geographers insist it does not exist. But he did find something else of interest: the Hawaiian Islands. While the area is populated by native people, Cook is the first European to set foot on the islands' lush and tropical shores.

Initially he chose to name them the "Sandwich Islands" after the fourth Earl of Sandwich, who was already famous for his discovery of the notorious bread-and-meat combo.

"It is paradise here," said a crewman. "The air is always warm. Food and water is plentiful, and the land is beautiful. We don't want to leave."

But they might have to. There is word that small skirmishes have erupted between the explorers and the natives, and the crew is expected to set sail for the coast of North America in the coming days.

Holiday History
Happy Valentine's Day!

By Cheryl Cherub

Today is Valentine's Day, the day on which lovers declare their affection for one another through cards and gifts. The exchange of love notes on Valentine's Day is a tradition dating back to the fourth century.

According to legend, Saint Valentine was a priest who worked in Rome during the third century. According to the story, Emperor Claudius II decided that single men made better soldiers than married men, and he outlawed marriage in hopes of building a stronger military base.

Valentine supposedly decided this was unfair and chose to marry young couples secretly. When Emperor Claudius II found out about Valentine's actions, he had him put to death. With that, Valentine became a saint and a legend, and consequently, a celebrated holiday.

The Explorer's Gazette

SEPTEMBER 24, 1806   VOLUME MDCCCVI NO. 39   PRICE: ONE CENT

TO THE WEST AND BACK!

Lewis and Clark's expedition returns safely; detailed journals reveal "beautiful" American West

William Clark

Lewis and Clark enjoy the view on their journey west.

Meriwether Lewis

ST. LOUIS, MISSOURI – After more than two years of trudging across mountain ranges, open plains, and dense forests, Lewis and Clark's expedition returned home safely yesterday. They are now the first explorers to document an expedition to the Pacific coast and back.

President Thomas Jefferson persuaded the U.S. Congress to spend a staggering $2,500 to finance the 3,700-mile (5,920 km) round-trip journey. With Captain Meriwether Lewis leading the expedition and William Clark as lieutenant, the so-called "Corps of Discovery" set out on May 14, 1804, from St. Louis, Missouri, with their initial goal being to find a water route from the Missouri River to the Pacific Ocean.

Lewis and Clark were also expected to document the various Indian tribes, landscapes, botany, and wildlife they saw

along the way. They were the first to describe the grizzly bear and the prairie dog.

"Nobody quite knew what was out there," said New York mapmaker Samuel Rhode. "They would be the first ones to find out."

The interest in moving westward was sparked with the Louisiana Purchase in 1803, in which the United States bought an enormous parcel of land from France for $15 million. The purchase included all or parts of the following: Arkansas, Missouri, Iowa, Minnesota west of the Mississippi River,

North Dakota, South Dakota, Nebraska, New Mexico, Oklahoma, nearly all of Kansas, the portions of Montana, Wyoming, and Colorado east of the Rocky Mountains, portions of southern Manitoba, southern Saskatchewan, and southern Alberta in Canada, and Louisiana on both sides of the Mississippi River, including the city of New Orleans.

"Once the U.S. gained all that land, people were eager to explore it," said New Orleans resident Priscilla LeBlanc. "It was a new world out there."

According to *Explorer's*

Gazette sources, President Jefferson believed that woolly mammoths, giant lava-spewing volcanoes, and other prehistoric wonders dominated the North American West. Not true, according to Lewis and Clark.

"They didn't find any woolly mammoths," said historian Frederick Time, "but they

(continued on page 2)

IN RECENT NEWS

Vice President Aaron Burr kills Alexander Hamilton in a duel. See U.S. POLITICS.

Hans Christian Andersen born in Denmark, lives happily ever after. See LITERATURE.

Nō'ə Wĕb'stər pūb'lĭshĕz fûrst dĭk'shə-nĕr'ē (Noah Webster publishes first dictionary) See LITERATURE.

Some of what Lewis found instead of mammoths.

ASK A STRANGER

What do you think about the new Louisiana Territory purchase?

"We bought it from France? Without a war? Is that legal?"
—Hester Price, tax preparer, age 25

"I can't believe Jefferson wasted 15 million dollars just to double the size of our country."
—Gunther George, politician, age 29

"I'm happy. I've always wanted to see a woolly mammoth."
—Drake Deuteronomy, seventh-grader, age 12

In My Crystal Ball

By Opticus, *Seer of All Things Future*

I PREDICT . . . Lewis and Clark will each receive 1,600 acres (640 ha) of land for their efforts . . . Sacajawea will get nothing . . . Lewis will become governor of the Louisiana Territory . . . He will die mysteriously in 1809, and no one will know if it's murder or suicide . . . Clark will become brigadier general of the militia for the Louisiana Territory . . . governor of Missouri Territory . . . and the superintendent of Indian affairs.

(continued from page 1)

described the western U.S. as a beautiful, plentiful place."

The team also documented about 300 new species of plants and animals, more than 40 Indian tribes, and was the first crew of white men to see the Rocky Mountains, a sprawling mountain range spanning 3,000 miles (4,800 km) from Mexico through the U.S. into Canada and Alaska.

A Native American woman named Sacajawea, a member of the Shoshone tribe, joined the group in Fort Mandan, North Dakota, and became vital in guiding, interpreting, and negotiating with friendly tribes. At some point during the journey Sacajawea delivered a baby son. This didn't slow her down, however, and she continued the trek with the baby on her back.

"She was just a teenager, but she was a big help to the expedition," added Frederick Time. "Without her, it might not have run so smoothly."

Traveling by foot, horse, and canoe, the crew crossed the barren Bitterroot Mountains. In mid-November of 1805, they finally reached Oregon's Pacific Coast, just before the winter rains. On March 23, 1806, they left Oregon and retraced their steps in exactly six months.

Compared to many of the missions that had set out to explore other regions of the world, Lewis and Clark's expedition was largely successful. Of the 48 men who set out on May 21, 1804, only one of them died, of appendicitis.

The Explorer's Gazette

NOVEMBER 11, 1871   VOLUME MDCCCLXXI NO. 46   PRICE: THREE CENTS

DR. LIVINGSTONE, I PRESUME?

Reporter finds missing missionary after four years of searching

Henry Morton Stanley

UJIJI, CENTRAL AFRICA – World-famous Scottish missionary and antislavery crusader Dr. David Livingstone was found yesterday after a 200-day search that cost thousands of dollars and enlisted the help of 2,000 men. He had been missing for four years.

According to an exclusive *Explorer's Gazette* source, Henry Morton Stanley, the Civil War deserter turned *New York Herald* reporter, found Livingstone living in a small village in central Africa. Livingstone, famous for his Christian missionary work and his published studies on the geography and people of Africa, was feared dead after disappearing in 1866.

It was a long, hard search for the missing explorer. During their quest, Stanley and his men endured malaria, dysentery, starvation, drought, floods, and swarms of insects. Several of his men died, and the *New York Herald*, which funded much of the search, spent thousands of dollars on the expedition.

"It took a long time, but we finally found him," said Chunga, a native guide for the search team.

Stanley located the great explorer yesterday near Lake Tanganyika, addressing him with words that are sure to become famous: "Dr. Livingstone, I presume?" He presumed correctly. However, Dr. Livingstone was in bad shape, weak from illness and short on supplies.

"It's a good thing we found him when we did," said freelance *New York Herald* editor Edward Scoop. "Who knows how much longer he would have lasted out there?"

Livingstone's most recent journey had lasted seven years. Altogether he has spent more than 30 years in Africa, his main purpose being to open trade routes while documenting his observations of the land and its people.

His time there has been invaluable. In 1855, he found the majestic 360-foot (108 m) Victoria Falls (named for the

(continued on page 2)

IN RECENT NEWS

Much of the city burned in "Great Chicago Fire"; more than 200 feared dead. See U.S. NEWS.

Rome is made capital of Italy. See WORLD NEWS.

Phineas Taylor Barnum's "Greatest Show on Earth" opens in Brooklyn; circus expected to be instant hit. See ENTERTAINMENT.

Crossing a swamp was one of the many difficult aspects of Stanley's search-and-rescue mission.

(continued from page 1)

queen) along the Zambezi River. The waterfall, on the border of Zambia and Zimbabwe, is the tallest in the world.

Livingstone was also the first European to cross the African continent from the Atlantic to the Indian Ocean. In doing so, he catalogued its wealth of natural resources and discovered numerous lakes, rivers, and other waterways for reliable transit, including the source of the Congo River.

An ordained minister, he has strongly opposed slavery. Ironically, however, his explorations have paved the way for the colonization of Africa by European nations.

Throughout his journeys, Livingstone has returned to England several times, largely to publish books on his travels,

David Livingstone on the cover of a bestseller about his life.

give lectures, and raise money for his missions.

In 1866, Livingstone traveled to Zanzibar to seek the source of the Nile River. While there, he got sick and consequently lost contact with the outside world. That's when Stanley began his search.

According to *Explorer's Gazette* exclusive sources, the famous explorer is still weak, but refuses to leave Africa. Reports say Stanley has given him fresh supplies and plans to travel with him around Lake Tanganyka for a few months, as soon as he is strong enough.

Stanley witnesses native people being taken as slaves.

FAMOUS
Livingstone/Stanley
TRIVIA

Ask your friends!
Ask your family!

Q: After Stanley asked Livingstone the now legendary question, "Dr. Livingstone, I presume?" what was the reply?

A: "Yes."

In My Crystal Ball

By Opticus, *Seer of All Things Future*

I PREDICT . . . Livingstone will die within eighteen months in Zambia along the Nile River at the age of 60 . . . Stanley will publish *How I Found Livingstone* in 1872, then give up journalism for exploring . . . He'll be the first white man to follow the Congo River to its mouth at the Atlantic Ocean . . . Stanley will help create the Congo Free State . . . and serve in British Parliament . . . and become a knight in 1899 . . . and die in 1904, happier to make news than report it.

Just Published and Ready to Read

If you liked *Alice in Wonderland* then Mr. Lewis Carroll's new edition,

Through the Looking Glass,
will reflect equally well.
Make an important date to read it!

The Explorer's Gazette

JUNE 1, 1886　　　VOLUME MDCCCLXXXVI NO. 23　　PRICE: THREE CENTS

DAREDEVIL EXPLORER'S DAYS SURPASS HIS "ARABIAN NIGHTS"

Sir Richard Burton's life reads like his racy books

Sir Richard Burton wearing a fez, a kind of hat worn by Arabs.

TRIESTE, ITALY – Sir Richard Burton, a British explorer, anthropologist, author, soldier, swordsman, and linguist, recently translated thousands of pages to produce a book that will rival his many and varied real-life adventures.

Burton, who was knighted by the Queen of England in February for his daring service to his country, recently translated the 16-volume *Arabian Nights* into English. The collection of stories—some of which have been criticized for "racy" material—includes such popular tales as "Sinbad the Sailor" and "Aladdin's Lamp." The nearly 1,000-page translation can now be added to the 48 books written by the accomplished traveler.

Burton didn't write the *Arabian Nights*, which is also known as the *Thousand and One Nights*. He translated the massive collection from its original Arabic language into English. The source of the stories, which have been passed down for generations, is unknown.

Muslims praying during the Hajj, one of the sights seen by Burton on his travels to East Africa.

Many would argue Burton's life is as exciting as the stories in his books—those he wrote and translated. After failing out of Oxford, he joined the British Army so he could study Oriental life and languages. He had already studied Arabic at Oxford and had learned Hunsutani (spoken in India) in London. As a soldier he went to India and quickly learned more Indian dialects, including Gujarati, Marathi, and Persian. At one point it was estimated Burton could speak up to 30 different languages.

Consequently, he was a natural traveler. With his proficiency in Arabic, he was able to sneak into the East African cities of Harar and Mecca. They were dangerous deeds, as Europeans

IN RECENT NEWS

Mark Twain's *Adventures of Huckleberry Finn* is published; teachers and librarians ban it from shelves. See LITERATURE.

Argonia, Kansas, elects Susanna Madora Salter as the first U.S. female mayor; some citizens outraged. See U.S. POLITICS.

U.S. President Grover Cleveland dedicates the Statue of Liberty. See WORLD NEWS.

were not allowed in Arabian holy cities, and those who were caught were executed.

"He went in disguised as an Arab," said Bartle Chinstock, an Oxford University professor. "He spoke excellent Arabic, so

(continued on page 2)

(continued from page 1)

he passed in and out without a problem."

In 1854, Burton had a new mission: to find the source of the Nile River, the second longest river on Earth, which supports almost all the agriculture in Egypt and provides water for much of Central Africa.

For hundreds of years, its source has been a mystery. In the second century, mathematician and geographer Ptolemy theorized that the water flowed from the "Mountains of the Moon." In 1770, explorer James Bruce discovered the source of the Blue Nile, one of the river's two branches. Burton wanted to be the one to find the source of the other branch, the White Nile.

With three companions, including John Hanning Speke and two other officers of the British East India Company, Burton set out through central Africa. Initially the mission failed, and a member of his team was killed by Africans. Injured, Speke and Burton returned home.

"Burton was a devoted adventurer," said Chinstock. "He wasn't going to let that setback stop him."

In 1857, Burton and Speke decided to renew their quest. After nearly two years of searching, they found Lake Tanganyika. They heard of a second lake in the area, but Burton, who had malaria, was too sick to make the voyage. So Speke went alone and found Lake Victoria, which he named in honor of the queen. The lake was the largest in Africa, and Speke believed he had found the source of the Nile. Burton disagreed. He insisted that Tanganyika was the source.

"They ended their friendship over it," said Guinevere Harvey, a friend of Burton's. "I don't think they ever spoke to each other again."

But Burton was mistaken. Lake Victoria was indeed the proper source. Speke returned to England and was celebrated as a hero for discovering it.

HOW TO BARTER

By Jenkins Yukon

Before Richard Burton was a "Sir" he was a spy. He spent many months undercover for his country. As such, he could not appear to be wealthy, so he became a master of *bartering*, or trading possessions, in local bazaars and markets. Money is a relatively new concept. Different cultures each have bartering traditions dating back thousands of years.

Remember: When bartering, the wrong comment can be considered insulting or even dangerous. Here are some of Burton's tried-and-true basics for getting what you want, at the price you want to pay:

1. Always keep a collection of items that others will think are valuable. In the early days of exploration, stones, beads, and sparkly jewelry worked wonders in trade. Know what people want.

2. Always act as if you really, really want to keep the item you are bartering with.

3. Show your less valuable items first. Never lead with your main item; let them ask for it.

4. Always start with a low offer; you never know when it might be accepted.

5. Always be willing to walk away. If the person really wants to make a deal, let him beg you to stay.

6. If you don't feel good about the trade, don't make it.

The Explorer's Gazette

APRIL 7, 1909   VOLUME MCMIX NO. 15   PRICE: FIVE CENTS

A BITTER COLD DISCOVERY

Arctic adventurers Peary and Henson reach North Pole after nearly two decades

The Theodore Roosevelt, their ship, with flags flying.

THE NORTH POLE – It took 18 years of planning, seven Arctic expeditions, and exhaustive preparations, but they finally made it: American adventurers Robert Peary and Matthew Henson, along with four Inuit assistants, yesterday became the first people to reach the North Pole.

With a crew that included 23 men, 133 dogs, and 19 sleds, the expedition began March 1 from Ellesmere Island in Northern Canada. By the time they crossed the 400 miles (645 km) of ice to reach their final, frigid destination, just six of the men remained.

"This region is virtually inhabitable," said arctic expert Wanda Snowdrift. "All your skin has to be covered or you risk getting frostbite."

Even with layers of thick coats and animal skin blankets, the cold is a constant threat. Years earlier, during another Arctic expedition, Peary lost all his toes to frostbite. According to exclusive *Explorer's Gazette* sources, he was wearing heavy shoes and socks at the time, but the cold still found its way in.

"He didn't want

The explorers' flag is planted at the top of the world.

that to happen again," said physician Barry Kold. "For this latest journey, he packed lots of warm socks."

Peary and Henson were the perfect team. With Peary's leadership experience (he has led numerous jungle expeditions in Central America to help plan the Panama Canal), he generated the funding and manpower for what would become a historic Arctic expedition. He even designed their special ice-breaking ship, the *Theodore Roosevelt*, which was

(continued on page 2)

Brrrr! **A bundled up Robert Peary at the North Pole.**

IN OTHER NEWS

Hudson Motor Car Company founded in Detroit, Michigan; designer hopes cars will compete with Ford, Chevrolet. See INNOVATIONS.

Months after its founding, National Association for the Advancement of Colored People (NAACP) membership growing quickly. See POLITICS.

William D. Boyce reportedly to unveil plan for Boy Scouts of America; program to provide leadership skills to boys ages 7 to 14. See TRENDS.

(continued from page 1)

made to withstand the ice-filled waters of the region.

Henson, who is an African-American, also has an impressive background. In the face of societal prejudices that discourage many black men from climbing to success in this country, Henson became a U.S. Navy engineer, skilled navigator, mechanic, and carpenter. He is also one of the few African Americans fluent in an Inuit language.

Together, the two explorers have conducted various expeditions around the globe. Before embarking on their trek to the North Pole, they led a mission to the frozen north side of Greenland, where they collected ancient meteorites for analysis.

"It takes a lot of stamina to withstand the frigid temperatures of these regions," Kold said. "You try living in minus 50-degree (-10°C) weather and you'll see what I mean."

The latest expedition was a marvel of planning. An entire Inuit village (Inuits are the people who live in the Arctic) was transported to the base camp, and the crew spent the winter gathering the proper equipment and supplies. preparations also included extensive observation of Eskimo customs, including the use of dog sleds, seal fur clothing, and igloos—all items that would be crucial in helping the men survive the sub-zero temperatures.

The men reportedly lived on a diet of pemmican (a food made from strips of beef and dried fruit), in addition to lard (solid animal fat), ice, and the slower sled dogs who may expire along the way.

The 24-man team headed out in March when the ice was at its most solid. A smaller team rode ahead each day and set up a new camp in advance of the others. When each smaller team's supplies ran low, they returned to base camp.

In the end, just six men reached the Pole, pushing through the final 133 miles (214 km) at about 25 to 30 miles (40 to 48 km) a day. After planting an American flag in the frozen tundra and spending about 30 hours taking notes, the crew began the long, hard journey back.

Said Snowdrift: "Getting home certainly won't be an easy feat either."

The Peary and Henson camp in North Greenland isn't finished quite yet.

It's *NOT* a Sled Dog's Life

By Fido Barks

Being a sled dog is hard work. The dogs are required to pull heavy sleds, which carry members of the crew and all their equipment. They travel up to 30 miles (48 km) a day through bitter cold and high winds.

The slower dogs are seen as a handicap to the mission—and as a source of good food. If a dog is slowing down the group, it is eaten by the crew. "Sure, they make us drag sleds and then eat us," said a sled dog who would not give her name, "but one day we'll be the first species in space."

Cold Enough For You?

25 of the Eskimo language's more than 50 words for snow:

* snow (on ground): **aput**
* slush (on ground): **aput masannartuq**
* snow in air/falling: **qaniit**
* snowflake: **qanik**
* air thick with snow: **nittaalaq**
* hard grains of snow: **nittaalaaqqat**
* feathery clumps of falling snow: **qanipalaat**
* new fallen snow: **apirlaat**
* ice floe: **puttaaq**
* large ice floe: **iluitsuq**
* small ice floe (not large enough to stand on): **masaaraq**
* drifting lump of ice: **kassuq**
* hail: **nataqqurnat**
* lumps of ice stranded on the beach: **issinnirit**
* snow blown in (e.g. in doorway): **sullarniq**
* frost (e.g. on inner surface of window): **iluq**
* wet snow on top of ice: **putsinniq/puvvinniq**
* smooth stretch of ice: **manirak**
* lump of old ice frozen into new ice: **tuaq**
* new ice formed in crack in old ice: **nutarniq**
* opening in sea ice: **imarnirsaq**
* ice swelling over partially frozen river: **siirsinniq**
* piled-up ice floes frozen together: **tiggunnirit**
* rotten ice with streams forming: **aakkarniq**
* avalanche: **aput sisurtuq**

The Explorer's Gazette

MARCH 8, 1912   VOLUME MCMXII NO. 11   PRICE: FIVE CENTS

AMUNDSEN WINS RACE TO SOUTH POLE

Victory for Amundsen; big chill for rival Scott

Amundsen's crew.

ANTARCTICA – It's the story of two men driven by ambition, rewards, and dogsleds.

More than a month after 39-year-old Roald Amundsen became the first man to reach the South Pole, his rival, Robert Falcon Scott, 43, froze to death shortly after reaching the finish line in second place.

Amundsen finished the race on December 14 of last year, when he planted the Norwegian flag into the icy ground. The race took him nearly two years. Now in Tasmania, Australia, Amundsen announced his achievement yesterday by telegram. He hasn't yet heard about his rival's death.

The journey to the South Pole started as a quest for the North Pole. Originally Amundsen said he would try to be the first man to reach the North Pole. He'd come close on other expeditions, but Robert Peary got there first, in 1909. Then the South Pole's previous record holder, Ernest Shackleton, stopped about 100 miles

Dog tired is one of Amundsen's canine companions. He and the explorer take a break during the journey to the South Pole.

IN RECENT NEWS

New 3-horsepower-engine cars. Old horses pull them out of the mud. See INNOVATIONS.

Woodrow Wilson, Governor of New Jersey, elected president. Promises, among other things, to end child labor. See POLITICS.

Maiden voyage of the *Titanic* scheduled to depart from the port of New York next month. Officials call the ship "Unsinkable." See TRAVEL & LEISURE.

(160 km) from the Pole—and it was then that Amundsen decided to switch poles, refocusing his energy toward Antarctica.

In an effort to keep his ambitions hidden from his competitors, Amundsen didn't tell anyone—including the members of his crew—about his

(continued on page 2)

(continued from page 1)

plans until the day they left, on August 9, 1910.

England's Captain Scott had begun his voyage two months before. But Amundsen's team quickly made up for lost time. He brought only sled dogs, which travel more lightly on the icy ground. Scott had been reluctant to use dogs, objecting to the common practice of killing weak dogs to feed the stronger ones. Instead he used Siberian ponies, which ended up slowing him down by getting stuck in the snowy terrain.

Scott also thought he'd maintain the lead by using the first gasoline-powered snowmobiles. He was wrong; the vehicles broke down almost immediately due to the bitter cold temperatures.

In January 1911, Amundsen's crew set up winter quarters at a location known as the Bay of Whales, on the Ross Ice Shelf in Antarctica. They had three months to prepare for their stay before the Arctic sun completely vanished, as it does each year between April and August. Even after it peeked out again, bad weather kept

them at camp, two miles from their ship. On September 8, they began approaching the Pole, steadily covering 930 miles (1,488 km) in three months.

On December 14, 1911, they reached the South Pole, erected the flag, smoked cigars, and left a note for Scott. They were back at base camp 99 days after they left.

When Scott reached the Pole on January 17 and found Amundsen's note, he was low on supplies and even lower on morale. Defeated, he and his team turned around and began heading home.

On their route back, the group was plagued with illness, hunger, frostbite, blizzards, and frigid temperatures. All five members died.

As for Amundsen and his team, whose expedition had been relatively smooth and uneventful, they were glad to make it out safely.

"Sure, we're glad we won," said crewman Jiles Icely, who added he's happy to get away from the Antarctica diet of seal and penguin meat. "But really, we're just glad we made it alive. Those are some pretty harsh conditions out there."

Learn These Often-Useful Norwegian Dog Commands

Sit = **sitt**
Stay = **bli**
Roll over = **rull rundt**
Hurry up! = **fort deg!**
Get warm! = **Bli warm!**
Come back here! = **Kom hit!**
Come back here now! = **Kom hit ne!**
Don't come back, see if I care!! = **Ikke kom tilbake da, se om jeg bryr meg!!**
Do not eat any of my seal blubber! = **Ikke spis noe av selfettet mitt!**
Watch out for that polar bear/penguin/hungry explorer! = **Pass deg for den isbjxrnen/den pingvinen/den sultne oppdageren!**

In My Crystal Ball

By Opticus, *Seer of All Things Future*

I PREDICT . . . The driven and competitive Roald Amundsen will try to set several more records . . . He'll be the first to fly over the North Pole in a blimp . . . He'll be offended that nobody cares about polar blimp records . . . in 1928 he'll die in a plane crash in the Arctic Ocean while rescuing another misguided polar blimp enthusiast.

ASK A STRANGER

"Will men reaching the South Pole change your life?"

"It's great, as long as I don't have to hear about what they ate."
—Clementine Ceecee, actress, age 45

"It's really the last frontier, isn't it? It's not like we'll ever get to the moon."
—Nigel Granger, chef, age 30

"I'm reserving my enthusiasm for whoever makes the trip in a blimp."
—Covington Harley, law student, age 23

THE EXPLORER'S GAZETTE

NOVEMBER 30, 1929   VOLUME MCMXXIX NO. 49   PRICE: TEN CENTS

HIGH AS A BYRD!

Richard Byrd becomes South Pole's first aviator

Commander Byrd returning in his plane after flying over the South Pole.

Amundsen congratulates Byrd on his accomplishment.

ROSS ICE SHELF, ANTARCTICA – Navy pilot Richard Byrd yesterday became the first person to fly over the South Pole, effectively spearheading a new road toward exploration of the daunting and frigid Antarctic region.

The round-trip mission, which instantly catapulted Byrd into the public eye as America's newest hero, took 18 hours and 41 minutes. Land-based missions to the Pole have taken several months to complete in the past.

"This is a major achievement," said Navy spokesman A.V. Ater. "Now we don't have to rely on treks through the region's sub-zero temperatures. Flying over the South Pole is far safer and easier than sending men out to brave the elements on foot."

But it wasn't easy. Byrd's South Pole journey has been a high-tech operation from the start. During the extended preparations for takeoff that began last January, the expedition team created its own small city on top of the Ross Ice Shelf, the largest ice shelf on Antarctica. The base, called "Little America," contained tons of equipment and all the provisions for research, including a hospital, photo lab, weather station, and several buildings to house people and supplies.

A crew of nearly 50 men set up radio transmitters to allow air and land crews to communicate. The mission used three airplanes, each fitted with cameras. A separate group was to trace the same route by sled and snowmobile.

"It's a tough place to fly," said aviation expert Harley Eagle. "Compasses don't work at Earth's magnetic poles. Byrd and his men were forced to rely on visuals."

At 3:29 P.M. on November 28 they took off. According to *Explorer's Gazette* sources, as the planes neared the Pole's high plateau, in order to hurdle its 11,000 feet (3,300 m) and had to dump about 300 pounds (135 kg) of food and supplies.

Such close calls are not for-

IN RECENT NEWS

Wall Street crashes, Great Depression begins. See FINANCIAL NEWS.

First Academy Awards announced; winners will receive a golden statuette called "Oscar." See ENTERTAINMENT.

Museum of Modern Art opens in New York City; founders wish museum to be greatest of its kind the world over. See FINE ARTS.

(continued on page 2)

Byrd's base camp on the Ross Ice Shelf in Antarctica.

(continued from page 1)

eign to Byrd, whose life has been nonstop adventure. Born into a wealthy Virginia family, his first international journey was to the Philippines when he was 12. From there he wrote letters home about his travels, describing faraway excitement and natural wonders. His fascinating letters were published by the local newspaper, and his story was picked up by the *New York Times*.

"He loved being in the spotlight," said childhood friend Marty Sparrow. "Sometimes I think he took risks just to get himself noticed. He liked the attention."

Byrd also liked to fly. That's why he became a Navy flight instructor in 1917, just 14 years after the airplane was invented. In 1926, Byrd attempted to become the first to fly to the North Pole. He returned to the base 15 hours later claiming to have reached his goal; but it was later discovered that he and his flight team had come just short of the Pole.

Shortly after this failed venture, Byrd announced his plan to become the first person to fly over the South Pole. Explorers had already trekked the region on foot, but flying over the area would give a fuller picture of the yet uncharted territory.

According to the *New York Times*, it was to be "the greatest feat in the history of aviation and exploration." A reporter went along for the ride and a film crew was sent to document the journey.

"This story had everything—danger, risk, triumph," said political commentator Harold Justice. "Everyone was waiting to see what would happen. Would he make it?"

Thankfully, this time he did.

The Ross Ice Shelf: What Is It?

By Victoria Shivers, staff geologist

Aerial view of Ross Ice Shelf.

The Ross Ice Shelf has been a base camp not just for Byrd and his team but also for past arctic explorers, including Roald Amundsen in 1912. But what is it?

Ice shelves are thick plates of floating ice surrounding portions of Greenland and Antarctica. They are fed by glaciers and snowfall and, unlike icebergs, are attached to land.

The Ross Ice Shelf is the largest ice shelf in the world, measuring 600 miles (960 km) long, or about the size of France, and from 600 to 3,000 feet (180–900 m) thick. Its flat, sturdy ground makes it a good—but chilly!—place for setting up camp.

The Explorer's Gazette

AUGUST 16, 1934   VOLUME MCMXXXIV NO. 34   PRICE: FIFTEEN CENTS

FAMOUS BIRD EXPERT SETS OCEANIC DIVING RECORD

William Beebe Discovers Fish, Not Birds, in Sea Depths

NONSUCH ISLAND, BER-MUDA – To find the answers to some questions, you've got to go deep. Really deep.

At least that's the motto of Charles William Beebe, the noted bird-watcher, who yesterday set the world diving record by reaching a depth of about a half mile below sea level.

But Beebe hasn't always been a deep-sea diver. Before his remarkable underwater feat, his expertise had been focused on higher things. That is, higher in the sky. Birds, to be exact.

Growing up, Beebe had studied nature in the wilderness of New Jersey. By 25 he was head curator of birds at New York City's Natural History Museum and its Zoological Society (also called the "Zoo").

Beebe has published several popular birding books with his wife, Mary Blair Rice. Together they traveled the world, journeying about 52,000 miles (83,200 km) across 22 countries in the pursuit of various birds in their natural habitat.

And then he looked down.

One day, while traveling by ship for a bird-watching expedition, Beebe noticed an unusual fish that had been caught in the nets. The fish was

William Beebe

dead, and Beebe decided it would surely be even more interesting alive. But how would he get deep enough underwater to see it? No submarine had ever gone below 400 feet (122 m), and no diver had gone below 525 feet (160 m).

He decided he would be the first. Initially, he aimed to dive 1,000 feet (305 m). If he could withstand the pressure, he'd go even farther. Of course he couldn't just swim to those depths; an unprotected diver below 200 feet (600 m) would be crushed to death by the weight of the sea.

(continued on page 2)

IN RECENT NEWS

Alcatraz, an island in the middle of San Francisco Bay, becomes a federal prison. See U.S. NEWS.

Gangsters Bonnie and Clyde and John Dillinger are killed by authorities. See CRIME REPORTS.

Ohio hosts first soapbox derby car race. See SPORTS.

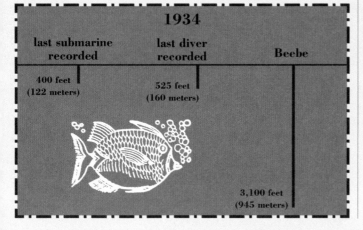

1934

last submarine recorded	last diver recorded	Beebe
400 feet (122 meters)	525 feet (160 meters)	
		3,100 feet (945 meters)

Beebe describes the bathysphere as "an enormous, inflated, and slightly cockeyed bullfrog." It has thick iron walls to keep its occupants safe from the potentially deadly pressure of the deep sea.

(continued from page 1)

Hundreds of inventors from around the world sent Beebe various plans for navigating the deep-sea pressure. The sometimes outrageous suggestions included everything from using huge accordions to operating giant mechanical squids.

But it was amateur engineer and fellow diver Otis Barton who created the *bathysphere,* a cast-iron tank designed to withstand the enormous pressure of the deep ocean. Named for the Greek word "bathy," meaning deep, it was this vehicle Beebe would use to plunge into the unknown depths of the sea.

Weighing 5,000 pounds (2,268 kg) and measuring about 5 feet (1.5 m) wide, the tank has 18-inch-thick (46 cm) walls with two portholes that look out into the water.

Air, electricity, and a telephone wire are connected to the tank by a single tube. For light—crucial in the sunless depths of the sea—the tank is equipped with a headlight. There is no bathroom or food on board, but the dives are short enough to make this tolerable.

After all the preparations were made, Beebe and Barton bolted themselves into the vehicle and were lowered by hitch into the sea about 10 miles (16 km) from Nonsuch, a small island off the coast of Bermuda. They dove a historic 3,100 feet (945 meters).

"It was dangerous," said physicist Marley Force. "If any water got into the tank, they would have been crushed like eggs."

In their dive, and other dives leading up to it, Beebe and Barton have documented countless living creatures never before seen, including species of eels, lantern fish, squid, and jellyfish. Beebe was also reportedly fascinated by the amount of light deep-water fish emitted to navigate the sunless ocean water. Prior to his discoveries, biologists weren't sure whether the apparent light organs on the sides of some fish actually emitted light in deep water; Beebe's observations proved they do.

The trip was sponsored by the National Geographic Society, and many of Beebe's observations and photographs will be published in *National Geographic* magazine, allowing the world to come face-to-face with the spectacles of the deep sea.

In My Crystal Ball

By Opticus, *Seer of All Things Future*

I PREDICT . . . Beebe and Barton's record dive will stand unchallenged for 15 years, until a solo dive in 1949 will set a new record depth of 4,500 feet (1,372 meters) . . . In 1958, the U.S. Naval submarine *Nautilus* will be the first to traverse the North Pole underwater . . . In 1960, the bathyscaph *Trieste II* will make the deepest dive ever recorded: 35,800 feet (10,910 meters) into the Pacific Ocean's Marianas Trench, the deepest spot on Earth . . . That same year, the U.S. submarine *Triton* will be the first to navigate around the world entirely underwater.

ASK A STRANGER

How will mankind's descent to the depths of the ocean affect your life?

"This could set off a whole new real estate boom!"
—Rory Bojingles, real estate attorney, age 60

"I don't think those diving suits are very flattering."
—Clarissa Ramone, grandmother, age 49

"I'd like to go along!"
—Lorenzo Whaler, student, age 7

Barton's Lucky Hat

EXPLORER'S GAZETTE EXCLUSIVE!

According to sources, Barton has some strange superstitions. Before each dive, he insists that he wear his lucky hat. One recent dive was held up while the crew looked for it; they combed the entire ship before Barton realized he was sitting on it.

THE EXPLORER'S GAZETTE

MAY 30, 1953   VOLUME MCMLIII NO. 22   PRICE: TWENTY CENTS

Mount Everest's Summit Surmounted!

Hillary and Norgay go over the top, overshadowing Queen's coronation

Sir Edmund Hillary

MOUNT EVEREST, NEPAL – It's a feat that some have described as impossible, an achievement that requires strength, agility, and a tolerance for bitter cold, biting winds, and perilous heights. More than anything, it's a test of human endurance.

And now, that test actually has been aced.

British mountain climber Edmund Percival Hillary and his guide, Tenzing Norgay, yesterday became the first human beings to conquer Mount Everest, the highest point in the world. Located in the Himalayan Mountains of Nepal, Everest stands 29,028 feet (8,850 meters) above sea level

Hillary, right, and Norgay, enjoying a much-deserved cup of tea after their successful climb.

at its summit. Airplanes have flown above it, but no man has ever trekked to the top of its steep and icy peaks.

"It's a hard climb, through frigid temperatures and with the ever-present danger of avalanches," said aspiring mountain climber Teddy Steep, who added that Everest's summit temperatures average about -36 degrees Fahrenheit (-38°C). "In the climbing world, it's seen as one of the most challenging climbs out there."

IN RECENT NEWS

United States military conducts its first and only nuclear artillery test. See U.S. NEWS.

Tornado hits downtown section of Waco, Texas; 114 people killed. See WEATHER NEWS.

Jonas Salk takes his best shot and produces first polio vaccine. See HEALTH.

Tenzing Norgay, Hillary's guide, during the last part of the climb to the summit of Mount Everest.

(continued on page 2)

(continued from page 1)

Hillary and Norgay had both made earlier Everest climbs during the past few years but had never reached the top. They finally succeeded, but they didn't do it alone. Led by Colonel John Hunt, Hillary and Norgay were accompanied by several climbers on their trek up the mountain; however, the famous pair did the last leg of the ascent on their own. No one was injured during the trek.

For Norgay, 39, Everest is familiar territory. He is a Sherpa, one of the mountain people of Nepal who often work as guides in the Himalayas. Last year he was hired by a Swiss team to climb Everest, but due to weather conditions they stopped just 650 feet (200 meters) short of the summit.

This year he joined a winning team. It was the ninth British expedition in 32 years to make the climb, but the first to make it all the way. Another pair of climbers had attempted the final assault the day before,

One of the first maps of Mount Everest made using photographs and sketches from an earlier, unsuccessful climb.

but Everest assaulted them first, and the lack of oxygen and a sheer wall of icy rock stood in their way, forcing the two men to retreat.

That rock wall, just 330 feet (101 meters) from the summit, didn't stop Hillary and Norgay, who found a narrow crack in the ice and crawled in. From there, they wriggled through as if they were climbing up a narrow chimney. When they sucessfully navigated the formation, which will now be known as the Hillary Step, it was an easy 290 feet (88 meters) to the finish line.

They reached the summit at 11:30 yesterday morning.

Hillary and Norgay have now become instant heroes. Reports of their climb have outshined the upcoming coronation of Elizabeth II, the first child of the late King George VI, who will take the throne of Great Britain on June 2.

"The real purpose of mountain climbing is facing the elements, testing your limits," Steep said. "Hillary and Norgay did this, and they'll forever be remembered for their remarkable feats."

In My Crystal Ball

By Opticus, *Seer of All Things Future*

I PREDICT . . . Hillary will have many more adventures . . . including climbing Mount Everest several more times . . . reaching the South Pole by tractor in 1958 . . . and leading the first jet boat expedition up India's Ganges River . . . He will also assist the people of Nepal by winning protection of Everest as a park and by helping locals build hospitals, clinics, and schools . . . He will live to a ripe old age . . . as will Tenzing Norgay, who'll die in 1986 a happy man.

Mountain Climbing Basic Gear

If you're climbing Everest simply because it's there, you'd better take what's here:

Helmet: To protect your head from falling rock and ice, or from the impact of a fall.

Ice axe: A critical tool for self-arrest, the art of stopping or slowing a fall. Also used for belaying (securing the climber) or anchoring.

Climbing rope: Generally used in lengths of 165 feet (50 meters). Dynamic climbing ropes stretch like bungee cords and are used to dissipate the shock of a fall. Static ropes are used to secure a route during long climbs.

Climbing harness: Worn around your pelvis, this is the primary point for attaching the climbing rope to your body.

Belay device: Attached to the climbing harness, it is used to slow a rope's speed in the event a climbing partner falls, or while rappelling (descending on a rope).

Carabiners: Small metal loops for attaching rope or other gear to your body harness and various kinds of gear to the mountain.

Pitons and chocks: Pitons are metal spikes with a loop at one end that are driven into ice to anchor the rope. Chocks are small pieces of metal with a wire loop that are jammed into rock crevices for the same purpose.

EVEREST: Just how high is it?

To understand Everest's enormity, consider that 29,028 feet (8,848 meters)—the height of its summit—is roughly as high as . . .

* Ninety-seven Statues of Liberty
* Thirty-four Transamerica buildings
* Thirty Eiffel Towers
* Twenty-three Empire State Buildings
* Four-and-a-half Mount Washingtons
* Twice the flying height of a bald eagle (eagles fly up to 14,000 feet, or 4,267 meters)

The Explorer's Gazette

APRIL 13, 1961   VOLUME MCMLXI NO. 16   PRICE: THIRTY CENTS

"I SEE EARTH. IT'S SO BEAUTIFUL!"

Cosmonaut Yuri Gagarin first man in space; historic journey takes mere minutes

SARATOV, RUSSIA, U.S.S.R. – It is no longer a thing of science fiction. A Russian cosmonaut has proven that human beings can survive in space.

Yuri Gagarin, 27, returned yesterday after becoming the first man to travel outside the Earth's atmosphere and orbit the planet. The entire orbit took 89 minutes. Door to door, the mission took 108 minutes.

It was a short flight, but it had big results, proving that humans can survive in the no-gravity, weightless environment of space provided they have the proper equipment.

The finding wasn't a total surprise. Russians had already launched a dog into orbital space four years ago. Laika, originally a stray, was sent into space aboard the *Sputnik* II in 1957. "If a dog can do it, it was pretty obvious a man could,

too," said the Russian astronaut Hileg Otto.

Before Gagarin went into space, the Earth was already being monitored by satellites that could orbit the planet in a matter of hours. But while those craft could send back information about space, they couldn't put a human sense of perspective into their descriptions.

"It is human nature to want to go where we've never been before," said Pluto Rungrin, a Moscow astronomy professor. "We went into space because we were curious."

Gagarin was selected just four days ago from among 20 other highly trained cosmonauts. Before joining the secret space program in 1956, he was a top student in the Soviet Air Force.

"His grades were out of this world," said one enthusiastic professor. "I knew he'd go

Yuri Gagarin on his way to the launch pad. He looks a little nervous.

IN RECENT NEWS

Berlin wall constructed, Germans divided over issue. See WORLD NEWS.

Roger Maris's 61 home runs beat Babe Ruth's record. See SPORTS.

FM stereo broadcasting begins, competition says "AM not worried." See ENTERTAINMENT.

ASK MR. DICTIONARY:

Cosmonaut: *n.* (Koz·muh·*nawt*) An astronaut from the USSR.

Gagarin and fellow cosmonauts enjoying some downtime.

(continued on page 2)

(continued from page 1)

places. I just assumed it'd take longer than 89 minutes."

Gagarin was promoted to major just before countdown in case he perished on the journey. "His rocket, *Vostok I,* is basically a 200-ton (180 t) bomb," said a military official. "He was brave to face such intense perils. You couldn't get me inside that thing!"

During the liftoff, Gagarin reported feeling heavy G-forces that measured six times the Earth's gravity. The rocket reached an altitude of 204 miles (327 kilometers) and a speed of 17,660 mph (28,260 kph). And then came the weightlessness.

"That's the part the astronauts look forward to," Otto said. "Without gravity you just kind of float."

Gazing out a small porthole in awe, his body floating in the rocket's compartment, Gagarin spoke the first words ever broadcast from space: "I see Earth. It's so beautiful!"

Gagarin was also the first person to eat and drink in a zero-gravity environment. Scientists weren't sure how weightlessness would affect digestion, but Gagarin reported no ill effects.

He didn't bring a camera with him on board, but he wrote in a log about what he saw, describing the Earth from afar and how its mountain ranges and coastlines made distinct patterns on the surface of the planet.

Gagarin didn't have to do much more than observe during his historic journey. The entire flight was controlled from Earth, and the capsule headed home on cue.

Four miles (6 km) above the ground, he ejected and parachuted to safety in a farmer's field. According to reports, an old woman, her granddaughter, and a cow, were the first to see him return to the planet.

In My Crystal Ball

By Opticus, *Seer of All Things Future*

I PREDICT . . . Back on Earth, doctors will check Gagarin for pain, illness, and alien creatures in his stomach but be disappointed . . . He will become famous worldwide as the first human in space . . . America will send up Alan Shepard on May 5, but not into full orbit . . . In 1968, during training for a longer space trip, Gagarin's MiG-15 jet plane will crash near Moscow . . . Gagarin Crater, a wide crater on the dark side of the moon, will be named in his honor . . . but nobody can see it.

ASK A STRANGER

How will a man orbiting the earth affect your life?

"I'll always remember those 89 seconds."
—Brendan Happnut, historian, age 58

"I thought Magellan already did that."
—Emily Mayer, fourth-grader, age 9

"I'll bet you mankind will be orbiting the sun in a year!"
—Maria Positivo, homemaker, age 38

Pros and Cons

REMEMBERING LAIKA

By Walt A. Crock

Yuri Gagarin was NOT the first to orbit the Earth! Laika the dog was.

Laika, who was a stray dog before she was captured and prepared for the space mission, was launched aboard the *Sputnik II* in November of 1957. The short-haired, spotted mutt served a very important function: She proved that mammals could survive up in space. Russian scientists were

able to read her vital signs from down on Earth.

Before Laika, other animals, including dogs and mice, had gone up into space, but she was the first to orbit the planet.

They'll Remember 1961 Until the Year 6009

By Alan Stamps

Obviously, this is a tremendous year. Because of space records? Baseball records? Motown records? Not at all. Because it's the last time for 4,048 years that the year will read *exactly the same* upside down as right side up. Digital clocks may make identical upside-down years possible in 2002, but those numbers look funny. Only old-fashioned numbers count.

The Explorer's Gazette

| JUNE 20, 1963 | VOLUME MCMLXIII No. 25 | PRICE: THIRTY CENTS |

Cosmonaut Valentina Tereshkova

HAPPY VALENTINA'S DAY!

Russia's Valentina Tereshkova becomes first woman in space

KARAGANDA, KAZAKH-STAN, U.S.S.R. – It was a flight that lasted three days and now has instantly become a milestone for women in a male-dominated field.

Valentina Tereshkova, who has been working for the Soviet space program for the past two years, made history by becoming the first woman in space. The 27-year-old cosmonaut returned to Earth yesterday from the third-longest space mission ever completed.

"Being the first woman in space isn't her only accomplishment," said aspiring cosmonaut Nadia Skyzania. "Being in space for so long is also pretty amazing!"

According to *Explorer's Gazette* sources, Tereshkova has now flown longer than all six astronauts flying for the U.S. space program combined.

But it's not surprising. The young pilot has been taking to the skies since she was a teenager, becoming an avid parachutist at 16. By age 24 she had already logged about 120 skydives.

It was around that time the Soviet Union, anxious to achieve another "first" in history (Russian cosmonaut Yuri Gagarin became the first man in space in 1961), wanted to send a woman into space. Since there weren't many women working as pilots, prospective cosmonauts were primarily chosen from among the nation's female parachutists.

In 1962, Tereshkova and four other women, including a female pilot, were invited to train as cosmonauts. The plans were so top-secret that Tereshkova couldn't even tell her mother what she was doing, instead pretending she was training for an elite parachute-jumping squad.

The 15 months of preparation for the mission included classroom study, parachute jumps, and time in an aerobatic jet. Throughout the training, it was never said which of the women would be chosen for the space flight; Tereshkova herself reportedly didn't know she had been chosen until the day of the mission.

"She knew she was in the running, but there were four other women competing for the honor," said Hira Barishnokav, a Soviet flight instructor. "If you ask me, I just knew she'd get it."

On June 16, Tereshkova took off in the *Vlostok 6*, two days

(continued on page 2)

IN RECENT NEWS

America mourns after President John F. Kennedy assassinated in Dallas. See U.S. NEWS.

Martin Luther King, Jr. delivers "I Have a Dream" speech. See POLITICS.

The Beatles top charts with catchy new tune: "I Want to Hold Your Hand." See MUSIC.

Tereshkova after completing a successful and groundbreaking trip into space.

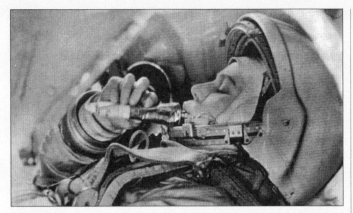

Tereshkova eats food in a tube during a training session. Yum!

(continued from page 1)

after *Vlostok 5* left Earth with Cosmonaut Valery F. Bykovsky. The two capsules orbited past each other several times, coming within 3 miles (5 km).

While in space, Tereshkova conducted numerous experiments concerning the effects of weightlessness. The entire mission was monitored by a Soviet ground crew who spoke to the astronaut by radio. According to sources, Tereshkova's radio call name was "Chaika," which means "seagull" in Russian.

After 71 hours, 48 orbits, and 3 days of live TV coverage, Tereshkova returned to Earth, ejecting from her capsule and parachuting to safety about 20,000 feet (6,000 meters) above Karaganda.

The twelfth human space mission had gone off without incident, but as standard precaution, 70 doctors examined Tereshkova for any pains or illness the moment she landed.

"Scientists still aren't sure how weightlessness affects the body," Barishnokav explained.

Shortly after Tereshkova's landing, Nikita Kruschev, the Premier of the Soviet Union, reportedly requested that she marry a cosmonaut so she can bear the first child of space-traveling parents. Word is Tereshkova is considering his request.

ASK A STRANGER

How will a woman in space change your life?

"Let's not forget that Laika the dog was the first female in space, six years ago."
—Alexander Sweet, astronomer, age 46

"Valentina, will you marry me?"
—Jason Jiles, sixth grader, age 11

"Shhh, I'm listening to the Beatles."
—Heather Honey, college student, age 20

Notes from the Future

AMERICAN WOMEN
WILL GO TO SPACE

More predictions from Opticus, *Seer of All Things Future*

Unfortunately, the Soviet female cosmonaut program will be disbanded in 1969. The next woman who travels in space will be cosmonaut Svetlana Savit-skaya, in 1982. The U.S.A.'s women's space program will then move full speed ahead, producing the following famous American astronauts:

Dr. Sally Kristen Ride, who will be the first American woman in space in 1983. She'll log six days in her first mission and eight days in her second. Many will criticize America for sending a woman to space 20 years *after* the Russians.

Sharon Christa McAuliffe, who will be slated to be the first teacher in space. She will hope to teach a lesson from space to be broadcast throughout the world. However, she and her six fellow astronauts will be killed when the space shuttle *Challenger* tragically explodes just seconds after liftoff on January 28, 1986.

Dr. Mae Carol Jemison, a physician, who will be the first African American woman in space, in 1992. She'll log eight days on a single mission aboard the space shuttle *Endeavour*.

Dr. Shannon Matilda Wells Lucid, who will log 223 days in space, more than any other woman. She'll also hold the American single-mission space flight endurance record: 188 days, on the Russian Space Station *Mir*, in 1996.

The Explorer's Gazette

JULY 21, 1969   **VOLUME MCMLXIX No. 30**   **PRICE: THIRTY-FIVE CENTS**

MAN STEPS FOOT ON THE MOON!

Historic event has major gravity though the Moon itself doesn't

SEA OF TRANQUILITY, THE MOON – After thousands of years of gazing at the night sky, wondering if maybe someday humankind would get there, man has landed on the Moon.

Following a four-day flight from the Earth to the Moon—a staggering 239,000 miles (382,400 km)—U.S. astronauts Neil Armstrong and Buzz Aldrin stepped off the *U.S. Eagle* and placed the first human feet onto the rocky lunar surface.

"It was a mission unlike any before it," said NASA administrator Sophie Flare. "Men and women have explored many places. We've gone to the ends of the Earth, the depths of the

Above: One of the Apollo 11 astronauts standing on the moon. Left (from left to right): Mike Collins, Neil Armstrong, and Buzz Aldrin beneath the landing module.

The event was viewed on live television by an estimated 500 million people.

Aldrin came out shortly after Armstrong, taking his first lunar steps at 11:16 P.M. The third crewmember, Michael Collins, did not descend to the Moon; instead he orbited in the *Columbia* while his colleagues explored the terrain.

Wearing thick suits outfitted with oxygen tanks, walking on the Moon was no easy task since lunar gravity is about one-sixth that found on Earth.

"It's kind of like jumping on

(continued on page 2)

IN RECENT NEWS

Roughly 400,000 music fans groove together at Woodstock Music and Art Festival. See U.S. NEWS.

First episode of *Sesame Street* airs; program claims to educate children with humor, silliness. See TELEVISION.

Beatles decide to "Let It Be"; announce they won't get back together. See MUSIC.

oceans, the tops of the mountains—but this is a whole new frontier."

The crewmembers of the *Apollo 11*, flying in the space shuttle *U.S. Columbia*, arrived into lunar orbit July 19, at which point the *Eagle*, a smaller craft designed for lunar landing, separated from the *Columbia* and descended to the surface of the Moon.

With the whole world watching, the astronauts landed on the Moon's Sea of Tranquility at 4:18 P.M. yesterday. Upon landing, the crew ate their first lunar meal and then began their exciting mission. At 10:56 P.M., Armstrong took the first step onto the Moon, proclaiming the momentous words, "That's one small step for man, one giant leap for mankind."

(continued from page 1)

a trampoline in slow motion," said aspiring astronaut Arthur Night. "They just bounced from one place to another."

The mission went as planned. After checking their ability to move around the surface, the two astronauts began collecting rocks and soil for later analysis. All together they collected about 47 pounds (21 kg) of surface material, all of which will be brought back to Earth.

To mark their achievement, the astronauts left an American flag and a steel plaque engraved with the words, "We came in peace for all mankind."

Then, two-and-a-half hours after they landed, the crew of the *Apollo 11* headed home. They are scheduled to return July 24.

"This is a great feat for America," said Luna Crater, professor of aerospace studies at the American College of Astronauts. "We put the first person on the moon."

The lunar landing has put the United States a step ahead in the space race with the Soviet Union that began in 1961, when Russia sent the first man to space. According to Soviet correspondent Marina Moonka, Soviet cosmonaut Alexei Iagnov, who was hoping to make the first lunar walk, was disappointed with the U.S. achievement.

U.S. officials have said, however, that it's our turn to push forward. "We missed the boat in sending the first man to space, and we didn't get the first woman up there, either," Crater said. "At least we're the first to make contact with the Moon itself."

In My Crystal Ball

By Opticus, *Seer of All Things Future*

I PREDICT . . . More trips to the moon in the 1970s . . . A Sky Lab in the 1980s . . . An international space station in the 1990s . . . And that hardly anyone will bother to watch those achievements on TV.

THE MOON: A CLOSER LOOK

By Dr. Star E. Gazer

The basics: The Moon, which goes by no formal name, is the largest satellite of the planet Earth and sits 239,000 miles (384,500 km) away. The side of the Moon that faces away from the Earth is called "the far side," or the "dark side." The near side of the Moon is covered with about 30,000 large craters that are believed to have been formed by asteroid impacts (the Moon has no atmosphere and therefore it has no protection from space debris).

"Seas" on the Moon?: The Sea of Tranquility, which is where Armstrong and Aldrin landed, is not a body of water. It and other lunar "seas" (including the Sea of Crisis, the Sea of Fertility, and the Sea of Serenity) are actually plains filled with rocky, solidified lava that rose from below the surface after a powerful asteroid impact billions of years ago.

If you went to the Moon: You'd have to carry your own air since none exists there. You'd also need a thick spacesuit to protect you from the Sun's radiation; the harmful rays shine right down to the surface since there's no atmosphere blocking them. And although that suit would weigh dozens of pounds, you wouldn't feel it. With about one-sixth the gravity found on Earth, everything is a lot lighter in the lunar world—including you! To calculate your lunar weight, multiply your Earthly weight by .17; for example, if you weigh 85 pounds (38 kg), you would weigh about 14.5 pounds (23 kg) on the Moon.

Because there is no atmosphere, the lunar sky is black even during the day. But, if you landed on the near side, you'd

Buzz Aldrin walking on the moon. The buglike machine next to him conducted experiments.

have a nice view of the Earth amidst all those stars.

A little history: In ancient times, many people believed the Moon died each night, and that its descent from the sky meant it was descending into the underworld. Others thought the Moon chased the Sun from the sky (and vice-versa) every sunset and sunrise.

Up until the 1920s, many people believed the Moon had a breathable atmosphere and that people could survive if living there (this is not true).

Today, some people refuse to believe the lunar landing ever happened, saying the whole thing was staged in a Hollywood studio. I say that is preposterous.

THE EXPLORER'S GAZETTE

SEPTEMBER 8, 1985   VOLUME MCMLXXXV NO. 37   PRICE: FIFTY CENTS

Sunken Luxury Ocean Liner *Titanic* Found!

Robert Ballard finds "unsinkable" ship using underwater robot

Robert Ballard

NORTH ATLANTIC OCEAN – To some it's the sacred gravesite of hundreds of people; to others it's a treasure chest waiting to be plundered. Either way, 73 years after its fateful first voyage, the ocean liner *Titanic* has been found.

Last week, undersea expert Dr. Robert Ballard and his expedition located the lost ship, which sank within three hours of hitting an iceberg on April 15, 1912.

The American and French crew found the sunken ship using a new underwater search robot called an Argo. The Argo, a device developed by Ballard himself, can dive deeper and faster than any human without the risks associated with diving.

Ballard and his team used the Argo to comb the ocean floor for *Titanic* wreckage. Using night-vision video cameras, a color camera, an echo sounder, and a sonar system, the device scoured the deep-sea terrain in a relatively fast sweep while allowing the crew to see the findings as they were made.

The Argo reportedly spotted the first pieces of the *Titanic* on September 1, near Newfoundland, roughly where it sank. There, more than two miles (3.2 km) below the surface of the ocean, the ship's rusted boilers suddenly appeared.

As the Argo continued to scan the area, more debris was uncovered, including empty serving platters, portholes, and wine bottles that had never been opened. The two broken halves of the once great ship were found lying about a half mile apart on the ocean floor.

"There she was, sleeping like a ghost, deep in the ocean," said Dr. Mary Marina, a professor of underwater studies at the New England School of Oceanics.

A spooky underwater scene of rust hanging like icicles from the bow of the *Titanic*.

"I don't think Ballard could find anything bigger than this," said Miles Traveld, noted expert on deep-sea diving. "He stumbled upon one of the largest maritime disasters in history."

But he didn't really stumble upon it. Ballard, 43, has been interested in exploring the ocean's depths for decades. He began his underwater career in 1967 when he was assigned to the U.S. Navy's Deep Submergence Laboratory at the

(continued on page 2)

IN RECENT NEWS

Mikhail Gorbachev becomes Soviet head of state. See WORLD NEWS.

New Coke released; goes flat quickly. See TRENDS.

The movie *Back to the Future* is big box-office winner. See ENTERTAINMENT.

Ballard uses underwater robots like this one to locate wreckages.

(continued from page 1)

Woods Hole Oceanographic Institute in Cape Cod, Massachusetts. There he spent much of his time in submersibles (small submarines) conducting underwater mapping.

In charting the geological formations of the sea, Ballard discovered tubeworms and other unusual life forms that exist near the deep, sunless ocean floor. He also found the largest mountain range on earth—far below the ocean's surface.

His interest in the ocean's natural mysteries ultimately evolved into his interest in its unnatural ones, including shipwrecks and sunken treasures. In his later searches, he reportedly scoured the world's waters in search of the lost and the unknown.

"The *Titanic* has been the most 'lost' thing in the sea," Traveld said. "For decades, the wreckage of that tragedy has been waiting to be found."

Ballard wasn't the only one searching. According to the international laws dictating the seas, anything found at sea is salvageable, regardless of its worth. The *Titanic*'s wreckage

THE "UNSINKABLE" SHIP:
TITANIC STATISTICS
By Will Float

When the *Titanic* left its port in Southampton, England, for its maiden voyage to New York City, its creators called it "unsinkable." At its launch, the ship was the largest passenger steamship in the world, measuring 883 feet (269 meters) long, 93 feet (28 meters) wide, and 185 feet (56 meters) tall.

There were 899 crew members and enough room for up to 3,300 passengers. On its maiden voyage, 2,223 people were on board.

The ship was nicknamed the "Ship of Dreams" for its massive size and for the many luxuries it offered. Many rooms were trimmed with crystal chandeliers, porcelain tubs, oriental rugs, and fireplaces; diners ate meals on fine china; and passengers could enjoy the ship's saltwater swimming pool, Turkish baths, and full orchestra.

is estimated to be worth millions. No human remains have been found.

But Ballard plays by his own rules. He reportedly decided to leave the *Titanic*'s watery graveyard alone, out of respect for the more than 1,500 people who perished in the tragedy.

"This is a graveyard," Traveld said. "Respecting that is essential."

ASK A STRANGER

Do you think artifacts should be removed from the Titanic?

"I don't think so. Those artifacts belong in the ocean now."
—Gwen Hopechester, retired school-teacher, age 78

"Sure! They should be in a museum somewhere. I'd like to see them."
—Jennie C. Currio, ninth grader, age 14

"That depends on who is doing the removing."
—Bennie Lawawa, professional scuba diver, age 30

In My Crystal Ball

By Opticus, *Seer of All Things Future*

I PREDICT . . . Ballard will be busy indeed . . . Using his Argo and JASON submersibles, he'll find ancient Roman ships, plus a who's who of other sunken ships . . . the ocean liner *Lusitania* . . . John Kennedy's WWII ship *PT-109* . . . Germany's WWII *Bismarck* battleship . . . And he'll also found the JASON Foundation to educate children about deep-sea exploration . . . The film *Titanic*, loosely based on the tragedy, will set box-office records in 1997.

The EXPLORER'S GAZETTE

JULY 5, 2002   VOLUME MMII NO. 27   PRICE: SEVENTY-FIVE CENTS

THE BALLOON HAS LANDED!

Steve Fossett becomes first to circumnavigate the world solo in hot air balloon

AUSTRALIA – After nearly 15 days in the air and several close calls, 57-year-old balloonist Steve Fossett landed yesterday in Lake Yamma Yamma, a dry lake in the eastern Australian outback, located about 725 miles (1,160 km) northwest of Sydney. He is now the first person to complete a solo around-the-world balloon flight.

Solo Spirit, Fossett's custom-built balloon, took off from Northam, Australia, on June 19. It then cruised through the clouds, reaching speeds of 200 miles per hour (320 kph). Throughout the trip, Fossett got about two hours of sleep per night, ate military rations, withstood freezing temperatures, and used a bucket for a toilet.

But there were some high-tech perks. Using a satellite computer, he exchanged e-mail, updated his Web site, and stayed in touch with his support team, including a personal meteorologist who warned him of any possible weather obstacles. According to *Explorer's Gazette* sources, Fossett said he spent most of his time playing high-stakes computer solitaire.

Minutes after completing the 29,602 mile (32,963 km) flight,

The *Solo Spirit* flying over Australia just after take off.

the American adventurer and millionaire spoke to the press about the historic journey. He described how his balloon nearly caught fire; how he came dangerously close to crashing; and how at one point he was forced to fly below 500 feet (152 meters) to avoid high-altitude winds.

"He set a challenging goal and he achieved it," said Australian ballooning instructor Roger Blimpy. "He has a tremendous sense of direction. I admire him."

IN RECENT NEWS

Spider-Man and *Star Wars II* are box-office favorites. See ENTERTAINMENT.

David Beckham voted world's best football (soccer) player. See SPORTS.

European Union adopts Euro as new currency. England won't join, they hate to lose pounds. See FINANCE.

Hot air balloonist Steve Fossett as he departs on his first-ever attempt to float around the world non-stop.

(continued on page 2)

(continued from page 1)

This is just the latest record-breaking journey for Fossett, whose achievement yesterday came after several previous attempts. Even before finishing the around-the-world flight, he had already set several balloon distance records, including the first trans-Pacific solo balloon flight in 1995.

Setting records is nothing new to Fossett. In sailing, he has 10 of the 13 fastest ocean passage records. He has completed the 1,100-mile (1,760 km) Alaskan Iditarod dogsled race, and driven in France's "24 hours of Le Mans" Grand Prix car race. He's competed in Ironman triathlons, which combine a 2.4-mile (3.9-km) ocean swim, a 112-mile (180-km) bike race, and a 26.2-mile (42-km) marathon, and he's swum the 21-mile (33.7-km) English Channel. According to recent reports, his next goal is to fly a glider to the edge of the Earth's atmosphere.

"Soon there'll be nothing left for him to attempt," said long-distance runner Timothy Longstride. "It's like he's got a checklist of all the great challenges in the world and he's doing each of them one by one."

Fossett wasn't the first to fly a balloon around the world; that record was set by Brian Jones and Bertrand Piccard in 1999 (see below). He was, however, the first to make the trip alone.

Consequently, yesterday's accomplishment is seen as one of aviation's last "firsts," putting Fossett in such lofty company as the Wright Brothers (first airplane flight), Charles Lindbergh (first solo flight across the Atlantic), and Amelia Earhart (first woman to fly across the Atlantic).

With this mission accomplished, Fossett said he does not plan on making any more major balloon flights, and that any other ballooning will be purely for hobby.

A Few Famous Flying Firsts

By Gracie Hites

June 5, 1783: France's Montgolfier Brothers make the first public demonstration of a model hot air balloon. They flew the balloon carrying a sheep, a duck, and a cockerel to show it was possible to survive in the sky.

December 17, 1903: The Wright brothers make the first heavier-than-air machine takeoff. They fly 120 feet (36 m) in 12 seconds.

May 21, 1927: Charles Lindbergh completes the first nonstop solo flight across the Atlantic. The *Spirit of St. Louis* flies 3,610 miles (5,810 km) from New York to Paris. It takes 33.5 hours.

October 14, 1947: Air Force Captain Chuck Yeager is first to fly faster than the speed of sound. His plane, an X-1, reaches 700 miles per hour (1,120 kph). He yells "yahoo!" but can't hear himself.

August 16, 1995: Super fast is the supersonic Concorde, which becomes the fastest commercial jet to circle the world, in 31 hours, 27 minutes. The sun never sets on the flight (so maybe they should keep serving breakfast).

The high-flying Montgolfier Brothers.

Did You Know?

NOT TO POP FOSSETT'S BALLOON, BUT . . .

The *first* successful nonstop flight around the world in a balloon ended on March 1, 1999. Bertrand Piccard and Brian Jones flew the 28,431-mile (45,755-km) journey from the Swiss Alps to the Egyptian desert in 19 days, 22 hours.

The EXPLORER'S GAZETTE

NOVEMBER 6, 2003   VOLUME MMIII NO. 45   PRICE: SEVENTY-FIVE CENTS

WHERE NO MAN HAS GONE BEFORE

Voyager 1 spacecraft heads for edge of solar system

Top right: Six planets seen by *Voyager*. Above: *Voyager* antenna allows the spacecraft to communicate with earth. Left: Jupiter and its planet-size moons.

PASADENA, CALIFORNIA – NASA officials announced yesterday that the *Voyager 1*, a craft launched more than 25 years ago to explore deep space, is now headed toward the edge of our solar system, marking the farthest outer space exploration that has ever been undertaken.

Launched in 1977 using technology far less advanced than what NASA has access to today, the journeys of *Voyager 1* and its sister craft, *Voyager 2*, have been very successful. During their unmanned missions, they have sent back spectacular images of the outer planets as well as information on the solar winds that exist in the farthest reaches of the solar system. No human has ever traveled that far.

And they're far from being finished.

Already located about 8.4 billion miles (13.5 billion km) from the sun (that's about 90 times farther than Earth), *Voyager 1* continues to cruise at a speed of about 38,000 mph (63,300 kph), with the *Voyager 2* not far behind. Scientists estimate it is now either inside, or will soon enter, what's called the termination shock, a turbulent region near the solar system's edge, where particles that have leaked into our system from beyond its borders are hit by fierce solar winds.

There is some debate over whether the craft has reached the termination shock, since

(continued on page 2)

IN RECENT NEWS

A Massachussetts-based company reportedly testing device that would enable paralyzed people to control computers directly with their brains. See INNOVATIONS.

To the Moon! Scientists say solar energy from Moon could be used for electric power. See SPACE NEWS.

U.S. Mint announces it will change face of the nickel for first time since 1938; new design to be released in 2004. See MONEY.

FOLLOW THE VOYAGER FROM YOUR COMPUTER!

For more on the travels of *Voyager 1* and *2*, go to this site: www.voyager.jpl.nasa.gov.

(continued from page 1)

the *Voyager 1*'s solar wind detector stopped working in 1990; however, most scientists agree it is at least very close.

"If the *Voyager 1* is nearing the termination shock—and we think it is—then it's on track to leave the solar system," says interstellar expert Celestial Storm. "We just hope it makes it through."

Scientists worry the turbulence of the region will damage or destroy the craft. "You've got to remember, this little spacecraft was built a quarter century ago," Storm said.

Past the termination shock, the *Voyager 1* will be met with a push of hot, fast-moving solar winds—an interstellar jet stream that scientists hope will propel it forward. If all goes as planned, the craft will break through the solar system's walls in about 15 years. It is expected to keep transmitting signals into the 2020s.

"We can't wait to see what happens," Storm said. "This mission has already gotten much farther than was ever expected."

The *Voyager 1* was launched on September 5, 1977. About two years later it was already whizzing by Jupiter, where it discovered the existence of sulfur volcanoes on Jupiter's moon, Io. In November of 1980 it reached Saturn, where it found complex structures in the planet's rings.

The craft didn't bother with the farthest planets, instead taking a northward shortcut outside their orbits in 1989. The *Voyager 2*, a slower but otherwise identical craft launched two weeks before *Voyager 1*, followed the more traditional route to Uranus and Neptune before heading toward the system's southern edge.

Perhaps one of the most spectacular images that was captured during their mission is the "Pale Blue Dot," a photo of the Earth taken in 1991 from 4 billion miles (6.4 billion km) away. In it, our planet appears as just a fuzzy dot amid a slate of dark, empty space.

In addition to sending back images of the farthest reaches of space, both crafts were designed to be interplanetary ambassadors in the event that they encounter intelligent life. The vessels contain a sampling of our planet's treasures, including a "Golden Record" carrying the sounds, voices, and images of Earth, and a map showing our third-from-the-sun location.

In My Crystal Ball

By Opticus, *Seer of All Things Future*

I PREDICT . . . NASA's *Galileo* spacecraft will end its mission at Jupiter, send back significant information, then head into the volcanic planetary core to self-destruct . . . The *Mars Probe* mission will land on the red planet in January 2004 . . . and send back news of life . . . The *Cassini* spacecraft will begin orbiting Saturn in July 2004 .

IT'S NOT ROCKET SCIENCE (IT'S MATH)

By Antoine Square, mathematics professor

Take out your pencils! Can you answer these space puzzles?

1. The *Voyager 1* is traveling at 3.6 AU (astronomical units) per year. How many total AU will it travel between 1977 and 2020, when it stops transmitting signals?

2. One AU is the distance between the Earth and the Sun—93 million miles, or 155 million km. Multiply by total AU (from above) and you'll find the distance *V1* will travel by 2020.

Now put down your pencils.

Answers:
1. 43 AU; 2. 14,396,400,000 miles / 23,994,000,000 km

THE GOLDEN RECORD WHAT'S ON IT?

By Wiley Noise

The "Golden Record," packed into each *Voyager* vessel, is an actual phonograph record (the technology of 1977) plated in gold to survive centuries in space. Designed to act as a "greeting card to the universe," the record was included on the craft in the chance that intelligent life should encounter it.

The contents, which were decided upon by a committee chaired by renowned astronomer Carl Sagan, are intended to be a sampling of the planet Earth. Each record carries greetings in 55 languages, sounds of nature, 115 encoded images from our world, and music from different cultures and time periods.

The record is encased in an aluminum jacket with a needle, and comes with instructions, written in symbols, on how to play it.

Above (top and bottom): Video/audio disc mounted on the side of Voyager. *The Sounds of Earth* golden record flying onboard *Voyager 1* and *2*.